THE BOOK OF
BEAMINSTER

And Local Village Life

BEAMINSTER MUSEUM

HALSGROVE

Title page: *Haymaking, c.1910.*

British Library Cataloguing-in-Publication Data.
A CIP record for this title is available from the British Library.

ISBN 978 1 84114 627 0

HALSGROVE

Halsgrove House
Ryelands Industrial Estate
Bagley Road
Wellington
Somerset TA21 9PZ
Tel: 01823 653777
Fax: 01823 216796
email: sales@halsgrove.com
website: www.halsgrove.com

Printed and bound in Great Britain by
CPI Antony Rowe Ltd, Chippenham, Wiltshire

Foreword

Photographs we keep in albums are primarily of ourselves and our families, to remind us of happy occasions at home. Other pictures we find in bottom drawers and attics, however, in a sense belong to a wider community because of the special atmosphere they evoke, the lost environment they portray as well as the faces of individuals we all remember. These rare pictures are the ones which Beaminster Museum has so carefully collected.

Beaminster deserves this photographic tribute for many reasons. First, as a small market town on the road between two larger communities it has sometimes been neglected, seen as a dip in the hills rather than a centre in its own right. Secondly, it has a number of important heritage sites, including an outstanding medieval church, which have given it historical importance and now attract visitors from all over the country. Thirdly, it has a thriving population and some of its key institutions, such as schools, new businesses and the museum, have recently had a renaissance and have given the town a new vitality, not least for its excellent food shops.

In the neighbouring hills and valleys are the dozen or more villages and hamlets that depend on Beaminster for their livelihood, with outlying farms which both supply the villages and rely on them in turn. History has touched all these smaller communities in different ways. Melplash and Netherbury were both important to the flax industry in Bridport, Broadwindsor looks back to the poets Wordsworth and Coleridge, Mapperton and Hooke have historic manors while Halstock was known for its Roman villa. Some of the photographs recall these earlier memories.

But the strongest images are those faces and places that some of us can still just remember from our childhood: the farmworkers, the scouts, the proud bandsmen and the owners of veteran cars, the turn in the road or shopfront as it once was, the noble Beaminster tunnel, the cottage now demolished. Many people here portrayed remain among our friends even if they are no longer alive. And this of course is the point of the book. We have an archive here of true value, that we can keep and enjoy and show our own children, as long as we are around.

John Montagu, Earl of Sandwich

Hogshill Street, c.1914.

Limbury Farm, Salway Ash, c.1970, photographed by the then occupant who had worked with a professional photographer earlier in her life.

Contents

Acknowledgements

This book attempts to give an historical outline of Beaminster and its neighbouring villages and to capture a bygone age through the medium of photographs. Beaminster Museum holds a fascinating collection of photographs and we greatly appreciate the kindness of those who have loaned pictures from family albums, many previously unpublished. Drawing on a range of oral histories and documents from Beaminster Museum and the Dorset History Centre, we have aimed for accuracy and apologise in the event of any errors or omissions. Some of the village sections have been edited by a local person or village historian. We record our sincere thanks to everyone who, since 1996, has given the photographs which form the museum's permanent collection and to the following for providing additional images and information:

Margo Allman, John Anderson, Aileen Bishop, Bridport Museum, *Bridport News*, Pat Bomford, Ralph Bugler, David Bullock, John Chandler, Jim Colborne, Fred Cox, Mary Cox, Mr and Mrs Derrick Crocker, Danisco, Sylvia Daw, Roger and Deirdre Dowle, Babs Draper, John Eedle, Chris Etherington, Jessica Featherstonhaugh, Sylvia Forsey, Dick Gilbert, Glamorgan Record Office, Tony Greenham, Sid Hawkins, Freda Hennessey, Phyllida Horniman, Jim House, Ann Hudson, Les Jones, Simon and Angela Mehigan, Anthony Mosley (photographer), Joanna Musson, National Motor Museum, Ernie Norris, Brian Page (Beaminster Cricket Club), Mary Payne, Bob Pearson (Beaminster Society), Philip Perry, Muriel Perry, Mr and Mrs Peter Pinkster, Warren Riglar, Murray Rose, Earl and Countess of Sandwich, Roger Skilton, Celia Smith, Henry Smith, Somerset Record Office, John Spencer, Emma Spurway, Ann Studley, Caspar Tiarks, Alec Walbridge, Bernard and Pauline Wallbridge, Audrey Welsford, *Western Gazette*, Ted Willment, Rupert Willoughby, Joan Wilkinson, and to those who preferred not to be publicly acknowledged.

Our special thanks go to Fred Cox, Aileen Bishop, Peter Williams and Penny Ruddock for their help and support and to Halsgrove for their advice and guidance.

Introduction

Beaminster and the surrounding villages nestle in the peaceful rural landscape of West Dorset in an Area of Outstanding Natural Beauty. The countryside is largely unspoilt. William Barnes, the county's great nineteenth-century rural poet, described it thus:

Sweet Be'mi'ster, that bist a-bound
By green and woody hills all round,
Wi' hedges, reachen up between
A thousand vields o' zummer green.

With no main railway lines and not a single mile of motorway it is the narrow winding lanes, the clay vales and the rolling hills which form the backdrop to life here. From Beaminster Down one can see the sea to the south and the lower land to the north. Some families have lived here for generations, their descendants still rooted in town, village or hamlet. Although fewer people are directly involved in making a living from the land these days, this is still a largely agricultural environment. There has been a significant influx of newcomers and it is hardly surprising that this area is often chosen by those who want to leave the rat race behind or who seek a peaceful retirement. Tourism plays an important part in the local economy and visitors enjoy the feeling of stepping back in time that the attractive town and picturesque villages afford.

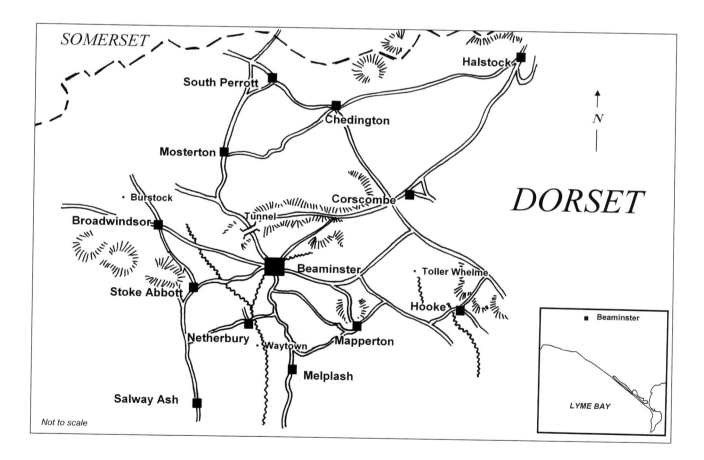

The memorial to Julia Robinson was placed in the Square in 1906, and is affectionately known as 'Julia'. On the north side of the shaft is inscribed 'In Memory of Elizabeth Julia Robinson of Parnham' and on the south side 'This Memorial erected by Vincent Joseph Robinson, C.I.E., 1906.'

St Mary's, regarded by many as the most outstanding church tower in Dorset, was built in the fifteenth century and embellished with 34 pinnacles that have recently been restored and strengthened. This photograph was taken in 1913, probably by Richard Hine.

A view of the St Mary's Church from Church Street taken in about 1900 and printed by T. Hallett of Beaminster.

Chapter 1

'Sweet Be'mi'ster'

On the hills north of Beaminster are Bronze Age burial mounds dating from around 2000BC, and south beside the River Brit traces have been found of later Iron Age and Roman occupation. A cast bronze coin of the Durotriges, the Iron Age tribe of Dorset, dated about AD50–70 was found in the garden of The Walnuts at Prout Bridge in 1963 and a Roman coin of Vespasian from about AD77–78 has also been found in the town. The earliest recorded version of the name Beaminster, around the seventh century AD is 'Bebyngminster', possibly meaning Church of Bebbe, a female personal name. The word 'minster' suggests the existence of a Saxon minster, but the site is not known, although a site near to the present church of St Mary's has been suggested. It is not until the early medieval times that we can be sure a settlement on the present site existed and recent finds suggest that the settlement stretched south of the current boundaries of Beaminster.

In Norman times the hundred of Beaminster was an area for the administration of justice in a district within a county. The Domesday Survey of 1086 suggests that the settlement at 'Betminster' was wholly agricultural with a population of 82 adults, which may mean an actual population of about 300 people.

By medieval times on the higher land there were strip lynchets – hillside terraces that were medieval field systems not unlike the terraces in Spain and Portugal. For several hundred years two of the main local crops were flax and hemp. The fibres were used for producing fabrics, sailcloth and threads. In 1284 a market charter was granted to the lords of the manors, two canons of Salisbury Cathedral. The charter states:

... to have in perpetuity a market every week through-out Thursday at their prebends of Beaminster in the county of Dorset and a fair in the same place every year lasting three days that is to say on the eve and on the day and the morrow of the Nativity of the Blessed Virgin Mary.

The purpose of the market grant was to encourage wool cloth and other industries, which led to the development of urban features. The population by this time was something like 350, no real increase since Domesday. The market would have consisted of street stalls for meat, butter, eggs and other local produce in the thirteenth century.

Leland in his travels (1535–43) described Beaminster as 'a praety market town... and usith much hous-bandry, and lyith in one street from north to south: and a nother from west to est.' By early in the sixteenth century the population was estimated at 500, and it more than doubled by 1700.

In 1625 a handsome Market House, built on stone pillars, was erected in the centre of the town, although there was probably a town hall before this date. There were also more permanent shops and a fine market cross that was probably late medieval and was described as 'an handsome cross, adorned with carved work'. The tolls from the Market House, the Shambles and the market belonged to the manor of Langdon. The Market House had been rebuilt and in 1818 a room was built over the market hall and a shop and house added at the west end. By 1850 it had become the Market House Inn but later the inn had reportedly become a nuisance and the inhabitants petitioned for its removal. Alongside were the town water pump and the stocks, removed when the Market House was demolished in 1886. A cattle and sheep market was held on 19 September each year in the Square. The site of the market was moved to Ham's Plot, then Whitcombe Road and eventually to Tunnel Road, where the name Fairfield can still be seen.

In 1906 the Robinson Memorial was erected in the Square, near the site of the original Beaminster market cross, by Vincent Robinson of Parnham in memory of his sister Julia. It is made of Ham Hill stone and local stone with a square central shaft which supports the roof. The pinnacles are of Portland stone and contrast markedly with the rest of the stonework; they once adorned Christ's Hospital in London and were secured by Mr Robinson when it was demolished. The design of the monument is similar to many old covered markets.

Early Worship

St Mary's Church, the town's oldest remaining build-ing was, in the thirteenth century, probably a cruci-form structure consisting of chancel, nave, transepts and central tower. Towards the end of the fifteenth century north and south aisles were added, the central tower was demolished and the magnificent west tower, nearly 100 feet high, was built. The church tower originally had many pinnacles that were probably removed during the Reformation along with many of the statues, although surpris-ingly many were left. The pinnacles were replaced during the restoration of 1877/8 but a gale on Sunday

Looking towards the chancel of St Mary's Church before the new rood screen was installed.

14 October 1877 blew them down and they had to be replaced again, at a cost of £1,200. Lady Oglander of Parnham House donated £200 with the remainder being given by local landowners and parishioners. Six new figures were carved in the restoration of 1877/8 to fill the vacant niches. The pinnacles were repaired again during the restoration of 2003–5.

There was a church clock from at least 1675. In 1769 a new set of chimes were added that sounded the quarter hours and at 6, 9, 12 and 3 o'clock when the hymn *Hanover* is played, having been changed to this tune in 1870. There is no clock face and the mechanism is now driven by electric motors to save regular winding.

The tower had a peal of five bells that were recast to eight in 1765. Today there is a peal of ten bells hung in two sets at right angles to each other to prevent damage to the tower. An inn in Church Street changed its name from the Five Bells to the Eight Bells, but did not update it again to the Ten Bells before finally ceasing trading.

Inside, the church had three galleries, the north gallery being added in 1657. The north and south galleries were removed in about 1750 and a new west gallery was added in 1796. The west gallery was probably where the musicians – called the 'gallery quire' – played and sang. In the churchwarden's accounts for 1767 there is an entry:

May ye 12th Gave Geo. Vile for playing the Bass Viol in Church 2s. Richard Symes in 1768. Gave to-wards buying a Bass Viol for Beaminster Church 7s.6d.

In 1828 new north and south galleries were added and by 1848 the church could seat almost 1,000 people. In 1861/2 the galleries were all removed, so ending the gallery quires, although their position had already been usurped by the installation of an organ in the west gallery. With the removal of the gallery a new organ was built in the Hillary Chapel in about 1865 and was replaced again in 1911. The 1911 organ was removed from the church in 2006 to make way for a new relocated organ, and the Hillary

Chapel was restored for use as a chapel.

The Hillary Chapel was built in 1505 by the Hillary family who lived at Meerhay Farm. The Hillary Aisle or Chapel appeared to be abandoned by 1848, when the Sunday School children were located there. This intrusion was resented by Miss Mary Clarke, who, claiming to be the owner of the aisle, ordered through her solicitor the removal of the children.

The pulpit was a fine specimen of carved oak of the Jacobean period. Until about 1840 it stood in the nave, against the second pier from the chancel arch, and was at that time an excellent example of a seventeenth century three-decker. The massive structure, built entirely of handsomely carved oak, comprised pulpit, reading desk, clerk's desk and clergyman's pew. The pulpit is now much reduced in height and on wheels!

Among the memorials in the church are those of the Strode family. John Strode lived at Parnham House in the middle of the seventeenth century. When he died in 1642 he left instructions that he was to be buried in Beaminster Church beside his father and mother. The family vault was rediscovered in 1856 under the south aisle; it had 14 lead coffins in it. There is a magnificent marble monumental sculpture of Thomas Strode and another in black and white marble commemorating George Strode and his wife Catherine. Both have recently been refurbished.

Beaminster had a strong Nonconformist tradition, with a congregation formed in 1662. The Congregational church was erected in 1749, enlarged in 1826 and modified at later dates. In the twentieth century concrete roof tiles were used, which caused the walls to spread outwards. The Beaminster Museum Trust purchased the building in 1990 and had it strengthened with an internal structure to which the walls were attached and a slated roof to replace the tiles. Beaminster Museum officially opened in 1996.

The Wesleyan Methodist chapel in Fleet Street dates from 1839, the Methodists having met in a private house from 1815, later in the back premises of the Star Inn and then in the Town Hall. The chapel congregation fell to a total of only nine by 1857 and no preachers visited the tiny flock. It was reopened with modifications in 1877 but finally closed in 1979 and has since been converted to private dwellings.

In 1848 an appeal was made for the building of a new church to serve Shortmoor, Newtown and Meerhay. It was anticipated that the extra trade, industry and accompanying employment from the tunnel would enable an expansion of Beaminster in this area. The foundation-stone for Holy Trinity Church was laid in 1849. The church continued to function until 1978 when it was declared redundant. The graveyard is still in use and the building itself is a private dwelling.

Close to Holy Trinity is the Roman Catholic Church at Shortmoor with two etched windows dedicated to John Munden, a Catholic martyr. There is also the

Above: *Harvest Festival in the Congregational chapel, c.1970.*

Left: *The Congregational chapel was the first of the Nonconformist churches in Beaminster. It is a Grade II listed building that now houses Beaminster Museum.*

Above: *Holy Trinity Church was built in 1849 for the expected enlargement of Beaminster and to serve Shortmoor and Newtown. The expansion only occurred in recent times and the church was made redundant in 1978 and is now a private dwelling called Trefoil House.*

Left: *The Wesleyan chapel, now converted into two houses.*

The Greyhound, possibly c.1900.

Above: *St Mary Well Street in the late-nineteenth century showing the King's Arms Inn. This street was the main route from Bridport and Netherbury before the opening of the turnpike road.*

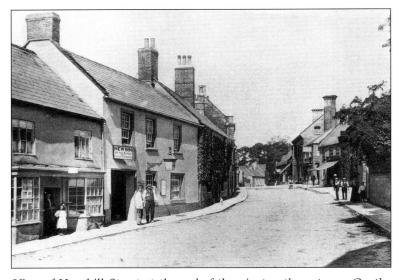

View of Hogshill Street at the end of the nineteenth century. On the left is the New Inn. The house beyond the New Inn was probably the former Green Dragon Inn.

Above: *The former Sun Inn.*

Below: *A view of North Street looking towards the Square. Further down the road on the right was the Manor Arms Inn.*

Wellspring Mission Chapel in Clay Lane.

Licensing laws in 1612 would not have been popular with modern churchgoers, or indeed anyone else. It was decreed that:

none were to tipple more than one hour in one house, beer was forbidden to be sold during the hours of divine service, and brewing on Fast Days was punishable with a small fine.

Inns and Public Houses

Beaminster was replete with inns including the King's Arms, first mentioned in 1619, the White Hart in 1636 and Red Lion in 1618 although the present building is of a later date. By 1729 the following inns were mentioned: Half Moon, Boot, Nag's Head, Crown, Dragon, Five Bells (becoming the Eight Bells in 1765), Shoulder of Mutton, Black Jug, Royal Oak, Cock, New Inn, George, Bell, and Queen's Arms, Fountain, Hare & Hounds, Rising Sun, White Dog, Blew Ball and Valiant Soldier. About the year 1750 there were more new inns listed including the Greyhound, White Horse, Coach & Horses, Swan, and Plymouth Inn, all in close proximity to the Market House.

In the nineteenth century there were as many as 13 inns – one to every 140 inhabitants! Some innkeepers

may still have brewed their own beer. New inns at this time were the Knapp, Smith's Arms, Bell, Sun, Manor Arms, Star (formerly the Bakers Arms), Alma, Royal Oak, and the Lamb & Flag – probably the house now called The Chimes in Shadrack Street. In addition there would have been several beer houses and cider houses where the resident was permitted to brew and sell.

In the late 1700s and early 1800s people used to go to the inn to hear the newspaper read. In 1854 the Beaminster Mutual Improvement Society was formed where 70 members were able to read the *Times*, *Express*, *Dorset County Chronicle*, *Bridport News*, *Punch*, the *Illustrated London News* and other periodicals in a small reading-room attached to the Town Hall.

A Local Archive

The Beaminster Institute was formed in 1896 with 80 members in Hogshill Street. In 1903, as a permanent memorial of the coronation of King Edward VII, the present Institute and Public Hall was erected and the Institute moved there; 'It was hoped that someday a Museum would be added to the premises to store curiosities of local interest'. The Institute held some items including an old Beaminster fire-engine, a banner of the Friendly Society, the original muster roll of the Beaminster Town Volunteers, an original

A crowd and two cars outside the Public Hall in the early-twentieth century, probably for an election.

programme of the Order of Procession at the opening of the Horn Hill Tunnel, portraits of notable local people, Dorset trade tokens and an original official brief authorising the collection of money after the fire of 1684. It would be interesting to know where many of these artifacts now reside. It was chiefly through the generosity of Mr Peter Meech that the scheme was floated; his portrait now hangs in Beaminster Museum.

Law and Order

The preservation of law and order was a necessary feature of town life. In the seventeenth century Quarter Sessions were held at Beaminster and the Michaelmas Sessions in 1629 required stocks, a ducking stool and a pillory to replace those that had been removed. In 1638 there was an order to set up a house of correction in Beaminster, but its location is unknown. The parish constable, whose only weapon was a truncheon, had the duty, after arresting a suspect, to house and feed him pending a magistrate's enquiry. Those who were arrested were fined, flogged or put in leg chains, the latter are now in Beaminster Museum. People paid to be present at the whippings carried out by the public hangman.

Night watchmen carried out the duties of keeping order at night. The watchman had a long staff, a rattle and lantern, as well as a bell attached around his waist – so he was sometimes called the bellman. He was appointed to walk the town from midnight to 5a.m. in the summer and until 6a.m. in the winter.

Constables secured payment for attendance at court ('For the attendance of George Swaffield and David Ian, Constables of Beaminster... at the whipping of Chas. Downe Gale, at 5s each.') In 1783 the

The present Youth Club in Beaminster, formerly the court and the police station. The cells are still in the building. It was established as a police station after the Police Act of 1856.

stocks were placed against the west wall of the Market House where they remained until they were broken up in about 1835. The last parish constables were John Guy and William Newman.

The Police Act of 1856 brought to an end the role of the parish constable. The Dorset County Constabulary came into existence and its first chief constable was Lieut. Col Cox from Beaminster. One superintendent and one constable were stationed at Beaminster. The magistrates used to have a room at the Red Lion Inn until the purpose-built police station was erected in 1860. This now houses the Youth Centre. By 1899 there was a superintendent, four sergeants and 20 constables based at Beaminster. Over time the police presence was dramatically reduced but, in 2007, it is expected to rise to four.

The Utilities

The first gas company was a private venture set up by Benjamin Coomb Porter in 1832 with a gasometer and works in the old tan yard to provide lighting for shopkeepers and residents. The Congregational Church was the first to use gas lighting in 1833 before the parish church in 1839. In 1836 the first public gas lamps –18 in all – were erected and the Beaminster Gas Company paid Thomas Newman to lay iron pipes to supply gas for the lamps.

In 1849 the shareholders decided to discontinue the supply because they were making a considerable loss. A new company was registered in 1868 after a public meeting and in 1860 the gasworks was transferred to the old quarry at Clampits along the extension of St Mary Well Street. The gas manager's house still stands as a red brick building with a bungalow alongside on the old site.

The gasworks was taken over by the Crewkerne Gas and Coke Co. Ltd in 1938. By 1947 the street lighting was changed from gas to electricity, electricity having reached Beaminster in 1932.

In January 1907 a new supply of pure water reached the town requiring the laying about 750 yards of pipes. The manager of the waterworks was W.B. Newman. The Newman family business survived in Beaminster until the end of the twentieth century when they were merged with a Yeovil company. Newman's works were at the corner of Hogshill Street and Clay Lane, and at the time of writing are scheduled to be converted into small businesses and residential accommodation.

Local Government

Beaminster Rural District Council was set up under the Local Government Act of 1894. In 1895 there was a Clerk, a Medical Officer of Health and an Inspector of Nuisances, later called the Sanitary Officer. Much of the former role of the Rural District Council has now been taken over by West Dorset District Council.

Beaminster Rural District Council, 1947. Left to right, back row: Mrs Ellis (Staff), Mr H.R. Newgass, Mr F.H.E. Moorhouse (CFO), Mr L. Samways (Housing Foreman), Mr C.L. Perry, Mr A.C. Lambert, Mr R.C.H. Studley, Adm Sir Dudley North GCVO, CB, CSI, CMG, Mr C.S. Coram, Mr R.C. Travers (Clerk of the Council), Mr E.D. Jones (Collector of Revenues), Mr C.C. Rundle (Sanitary and Building Inspector), Mr J.W.R. Newman (Manager, Beaminster Water Supplies), Mr W.R. Riglar (Staff), Miss G. Travers (Staff); middle row: Dr A. Armit (MOH), Lieut Col T.A. Headlam, Hon J.W. Best OBE, Revd O.R. Powell-Evans, SSF, Col W.L.S. Casson, Adm Sir V.A. Critchley VC, KCB, DSC, Mr E.J. Henson, Mr J.C. Shoobridge MBE, Mr R.E. Ashford, Mr M.L. Skyrm, MA (Beaminster), Mr E.J. Bailey, Mr M.A. Pinney, Mr J.S. Bugler, Mr S.J. Stenhouse, Comdr Sir Francis Peto Bart, RN, Mr S. Chaffey; front row: Captain G. Walker, Lieut Col C.J. Troyte-Bullock DSO, Mrs le Poer French, Mr T.A. Case, Lady Lilian Digby, Mr J.C. Davy, Captain N.H. Carter, RN (Former Chairman), Col G.A. Pinney DL, JP (Chairman), Mr Robert Leigh (Former Clerk), Mr J.R. Wyatt, Mr E.J.S. Holloway, R. Pease, Mr Robert Hine (Beaminster), Mrs E.F. Holder, Mr F.T. Bugler (Beaminster).

Beaminster Today

In 2007 the population stands at about 3,500, almost the same as in 1841. In the nineteenth century each dwelling would have been occupied by up to ten people but today this figure is closer to two or three which accounts for the increase in houses. Pattle, Fairfield, Gerrards Green were developed and new modern housing has extended along the Tunnel Road.

Right: *Beaminster Town Council, 1983.* Left to right, standing: *David Jones, Cecil Tolman, Glynis Watt, Ralph Bugler, Harry Walters, Vera Ivory, David Barrett, John Spooner, Donald Berry;* sitting: *Elizabeth Blair (Clerk), Norman Welsford (Chairman), Janet Page (Vice Chairman).*

Fleet Street, before 1900.

Right: *Cottage at Newtown, c.1900.* Left to right: *Ada Bugler, Mrs Bugler, Mr Bugler, Mr Curtis. It is thought that Mrs Bugler took in washing from the families such as the Daniels, Hines, Pims and Tolmans. She collected it with a pony and cart.*

A group of people outside Horn Park Farm, c.1910-20.

Broadwindsor's Story

Broadwindsor lies some 2½ miles to the north-west of Beaminster and is surrounded by the small villages and hamlets of Little Windsor, Drimpton, Dibberford, Coles Cross, Childhay, Burstock, Hursey, Birdsmoorgate and Blackdown. Dorset's two highest points, Lewesdon Hill and Pilsdon Pen, stand above the village; called The Cow and The Calf they were said to form landmarks for sailors. The Revd William Crowe in his poem *Lewesdon Hill* described the view in the 1780s:

Variegated scene, of hills
And woods and fruitful vales, and villages
Half-hid in tufted orchards, and the sea
Boundless and studded thick with many a sail.

The Domesday Survey of 1086 records that the manor was held by Hunger, the son of a servant in the Norman King William's household. Nearby Childhay was held by a Saxon called Osmund the Baker and Little Windsor by another Norman, William de Mohun. Shortly after this time Burstock was given to Forde Abbey, which also held parcels of land at Fursmore (Birdsmoorgate). Later lords of the manor of Broadwindsor included Gervase de Windesore and John de Windesores (1293), Adam de Stratton (1264), John Everard, and Sir Hugh Courtenay (1331). It remained in the Courtenay family for the next 200 years.

Broadwindsor men were involved in Perkin Warbeck's failed attempt to take Henry VII's throne in 1498. Warbeck was executed but his supporters got off more lightly with the tithings of Drimpton and Broadwindsor fined £10 apiece for their part in the rebellion. John Waller, John Bragge and John Studley had to pay 20s. each.

Fears of insurrection prompted Henry VIII to set up local militias and the muster rolls that followed recorded what sort of fighting capability was available to the King. Broadwindsor had 38 able-bodied men at this time. The parish was expected to provide 'a harnys (a suit of armour), a bowe and a sheaf of arrowes to serve the King'. The equipment that each man had to make available was based on his status. Most of the inhabitants were 'able billmen' and they were each expected to produce a billhook. A few were archers and they had to supply their own bows and arrows. Thomas Bagg and several other bowmen had 'a sallet and a pair of splents' (a helmet and elbow guards) and three men had their own suits of armour.

A Royal Escape

The Civil War made its mark on village history. In 1649 King Charles was executed and his son, Charles II, overcome by Oliver Cromwell at the Battle of Worcester, fled for his life. Failing to board a ship at Bristol he decided to make his way to Trent, the house of Colonel Francis Wyndham, a distinguished Royalist. Plans were made for Charles to go to an inn at Charmouth and wait there for the arrival of a small boat on Charmouth beach which would take him out to a ship sailing across the Channel from Lyme. Although the tide was right at midnight no boat came; it seems that the boatman's wife, fearing what might happen if her husband was caught helping Royalists, locked him in his room so he couldn't leave the house.

Meanwhile Charles set out for Bridport to await further news but the town was full of Cromwell's Roundheads and it was no place to stay. He decided to return to Trent taking the London road then turning off for safety and heading inland. The route is uncertain but traditionally it was considered to be up Lee Lane towards Bradpole. More probably he travelled through wooded country around Powerstock, Hooke and Wraxall.

As darkness fell the King's party found themselves at the Castle Inn at Broadwindsor. The landlord was known to Colonel Wyndham and considered trustworthy so the group chose to stay there for the night. Charles was shown to the attic, it being the most private room in the house. Suddenly the peace was shattered by the arrival of the village constable with a troop of Roundhead soldiers who wanted to billet at the inn. They occupied all the lower rooms and corridors leaving Charles trapped above. Their attention was distracted when one of the women travelling with the soldiers went into labour in the kitchen. This caused an uproar as the local people feared that the mother and baby would be left there after the troops had gone, becoming a financial burden on the village. A fierce argument broke out between parish officials and the soldiers which lasted until morning. The King had no sleep that night but was safe once the soldiers had left and was able to continue to Trent, eventually making his way to the Sussex coast and escaping to France. Nothing is known of the fate of the baby who unwittingly saved him!

At the time of this adventure the inn was called

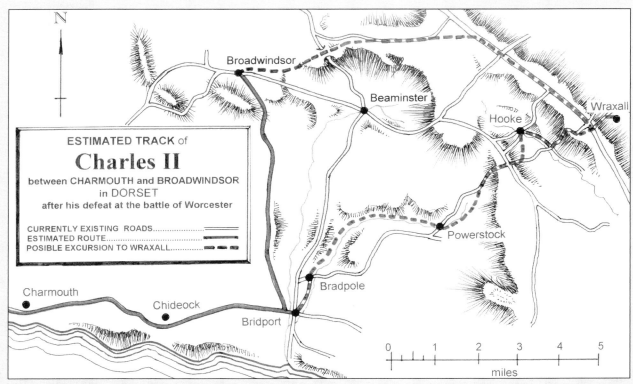

Charles II's journey from Charmouth to Broadwindsor.

the Castle and only later was it renamed the George. Part of the building, including the King's Room, was destroyed by fire in 1856. A tablet on the wall of the adjacent cottage, a private dwelling, marks the site of Charles II's stay.

Prominent Vicars

One notable seventeenth-century resident was Dr Thomas Fuller, a young and already well-known preacher and author, who became vicar in 1634. It is said that he was so effective a preacher that he spoke from the steps of the church because there was not enough room to accommodate the large congregation inside. He is best remembered now for his book *The Worthies of England*. The pulpit from which he preached, although much restored, retains the carved oak panelling of the period. It was described by Sir Frederick Treves in 1906 as 'elaborately carved with floral designs, and if not as quaint as the preacher, is at least as florid'!

His successor, John Pinney, was a Puritan and a member of the local landowning family. He was highly regarded by his parishioners but in August 1662 he was ejected from the living because of harsh legislation against Puritans. He became a travelling preacher and was imprisoned twice. He spent much time in Dublin but also preached at secret dissenters' meetings at Crewkerne, Bridport, Bettiscombe and Blackdown.

On the site of the old meeting house at Blackdown now stands Holy Trinity Church and the burial ground contains the graves of many

dissenters. In 1685 his youngest son, Azariah, became involved in the Monmouth Rebellion. Azariah was gaoled at Dorchester and sentenced to death but after bribes had been paid he was allowed to go into exile in the Leeward Islands as a free man, where he made a considerable fortune. As the family fortunes and status improved the Pinney's played an increasingly important part in county life.

A Place of Poetry

In the mid-eighteenth century John Frederick Pinney, grandson of Azariah, built Racedown Lodge on the site of an old farmstead. It was here that the poet William Wordsworth came to stay rent-free with his sister Dorothy in 1795. The poet Samuel Taylor Coleridge later came to Racedown to stay with them for a time. Wordsworth settled down to write *The Borderers* and *Guilt and Sorrow*. In her journal Dorothy wrote an evocative description of Broadwindsor:

We walk about two hours every morning – we have many pleasant walks about us, and what a great advantage, the roads are of a sandy kind and almost always dry. We can see the sea 150 or 200 yards from the door, and at a little distance have an extensive view terminated by the sea seen through different openings of the unequal hills. We have not the warmth and luxuriance of Devonshire, though there is no want either of wood or cultivation, but the trees appear to suffer from the sea blasts. We have hills, which, seen from a distance, almost take on the character of mountains, some cultivated nearly to their summits, others in their wild state, covered with furze and broom. These delight me the most as they remind me of our native wilds.

The surroundings which the Wordsworths found so congenial also harboured great poverty. In 1786 Samuel Ewens sold a house and gardens next to the old manse in West Street to the parish for use as a workhouse for over 40 inmates.

Nineteenth-Century Trades

At the start of the nineteenth century Broadwindsor was a flourishing place. Employment was chiefly in agriculture and there was work to be found at a sailcloth factory on the site of the present-day Yarn Barton which employed 30–40 hands; some were not local people and were regarded as pretty rough types. Cottagers undertook hand-loom weaving in their homes and it was said that it 'was seldom possible to walk down the street without hearing the click of the weaver's shuttle'.

In 1841, when the population stood at just over 1,600, the census also records saddlers, thatchers, blacksmiths, carpenters and masons. There were dressmakers and tailors, milliners, innkeepers and shopkeepers, a baker and a butcher, a nurseryman, a tallow chandler and a wheelwright, shoemakers and a glove cutter, a hairdresser and a washerwoman, a clock repairer, a sieve maker and a cooper as well as domestic servants. Folk higher up the social scale included a schoolmaster and a schoolmistress, a surveyor, two surgeons, an apothecary and those of independent means as well as a clergyman.

Vicars of Note

George Denison was vicar from 1838 to 1845. He built a substantial new vicarage, now known as Broadwindsor House, as well as a new school on the site of Thomas Fuller's old vicarage in Broadwindsor and a small church at Blackdown. He borrowed money to undertake these projects, writing many years later 'I have been half-ruined ever since'. The vicarage with its grounds and stables cost about £3,000 and the school and Blackdown Church £1,000 each. He conducted classes for adults on a Sunday so on their one day off the hard-working factory hands came to be taught reading and writing although they were not considered able enough for 'summing'. He earned the gratitude of the villagers who were alarmed by the rick-burning and rioting in the troubled 1840s by applying to the Home Office for one of the recently established 'Peelers' (a policeman) who arrived complete with 'belt, bludgeon, dark lantern

and small dog'.

Denison's successor was Dr Solomon C. Malan (1845–85). A highly talented man, sometimes described as a genius, he specialised in ancient oriental languages, wrote numerous articles and books on a wide variety of topics and travelled extensively. These activities do not seem to have detracted from his 40 years work in Broadwindsor. He supervised the building of the Blackdown school and schoolhouse and in 1867 was responsible for building the church at Drimpton. There was no village doctor and Malan treated minor ailments in his kitchen, with only the most serious cases being sent to the doctor in Beaminster. He visited his parishioners regularly and often helped them with gifts of money and food.

His enthusiasm for reorganisation resulted in the wholesale demolition and rebuilding of the parish church of St John the Baptist in 1868, financially supported by his son, Major C. Malan. This redevelopment did away with the old box pews and two galleries. The 'gallery quire', with their fiddles, flutes and violoncello was dispensed with and replaced by a harmonium – indeed, Thomas Hardy described such an event in *Under the Greenwood Tree*.

The Congregational Church was built in West Street in 1821 and there was also a Gospel Hall in the High Street.

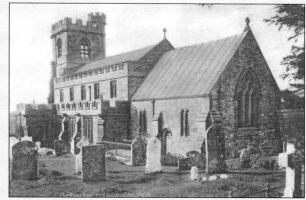

Above: *Broadwindsor church, c.1909.*

Below: *Broadwindsor church, interior.*

A Crime of Passion?

In 1865 Broadwindsor gained unwanted prominence when a local woman, Martha Brown, was sentenced to hang for murder. Martha, who lived at Birdsmoorgate, was married to John Brown, some 15 years her junior. On discovering that he was having an affair with Mary Davis from the same village she killed him with a hatchet in a fit of jealous rage. As the wronged wife she was regarded with some sympathy but the jury at Dorchester were quick to find her guilty. The folk of Broadwindsor were reported to have stoned the 'other woman' when she passed through the village on her way to watch her rival die and some said she should have hanged instead for leading John astray.

A newspaper of the time printed Martha's final confession which included the words, 'As soon as I had done it, I wished I had not, and would have given the world not to have done it.' Martha Brown was the last woman to be publicly hanged in Dorset and Thomas Hardy, then only a youth, witnessed the macabre sight of her corpse swaying on the rope outside Dorchester Gaol.

Above: *Broadwindsor Post Office, c.1909. The postman (right) is Mr Swaffield, the lady in the doorway is Mrs Pope. The couple on bicycles lived at Rock House, Broadwindsor and cycled to Crewkerne to fetch their newspapers.*

Right: *Broadwindsor's PC Churchill with four children (left), c.1906.*

Below: *Street scene, outside the Cross Keys, c.1900.*

Below, right: *The Cross Keys Inn in the High Street, c.1900.*

Horses in the Square for requisitioning, August 1914.

Celebrating Tommy Ackerman's return from the Boer War, c.1902.

The fête, 1930. 'Loveday, Boucher, Queen Studley, and Ma'.

Festivities and Traditions

Village life continued its normal round of hard work relieved by occasional festivities. Club Day was a holiday for everyone. One eyewitness account by Theophilus Bartlett describes flower garlands and flags decorating the village and 'In the centre of the Square was planted a large fir tree... and soon the Square was filled with stalls of ginger Bread, Shooting boards, etc.' Broadwindsor's Club-Walking hymn was sung which included the words:

> This is a joyful day O Lord
> To meet in this thy place
> May this Society obtain
> Thy Mercy and Thy Grace.

The club marched behind the Beaminster Band,

held a church service, picnicked on Pilsdon Pen and ended with a meal of roast beef and plum pudding followed by music and dancing in a large tent.

Postwar Broadwindsor

The first council-houses were built between the wars, with more following after 1945. A reminder of the Second World War in the form of a 'dragon's tooth' (an anti-tank concrete block) stands at the entrance of today's Broadwindsor Craft Centre on the road to Beaminster. Mains electricity had arrived in 1935 but mains water not until 1962. A new school and the Comrades Hall, which replaced the old British Legion Hall, were both opened in 1968. As is true almost every-where, modern housing has extended the village.

Above: *Broadwindsor WI Drama Group, c.1970. Third from right: Pauline Saint; second from right: Mary Broomfield; far right: Mary Frampton.*

Above: *Broadwindsor WI, 1937.*

Above right: *View of Broadwaindsor from the west.*

Above: *Broadwindsor High Street.*

Below: *Dunster Hayes, Hursey, c.1951. It was sold in 1951 to Albert William Denning of Paddocks Farm, Broadwindsor for £2,000 with 2¼ acres of land.*

Tudor's Stores, c.1930-40.

Chapter 2

Names and Faces

The character of a town or village comes from its people. It is through them that the natural landscape has been changed to meet their needs; it is the inhabitants who have created the buildings and structures that make the place what it is. Over the centuries Beaminster has had its share of people of wealth and influence, people who worked the land and people who owned the land, people who built their businesses and people who were employed by them – all who made Beaminster what it is today. The names and deeds of some Beaminsterians are known to us and some of these individuals made their mark in the wider world.

Joseph and Benjamin Parsons

In the mid-1600s two Beaminster boys, Joseph and Benjamin Parsons, left their home in East Street for the New World. Joseph settled in what became Springfield in Connecticut and started trading in furs. He soon prospered and was appointed to public office. After moving to another town, his wife Mary faced allegations of witchcraft. Joseph took her accuser to law and won the case. Their fortunes continued to improve but in 1674 Mary was again named as a witch and was sent to prison in Salem until her trial took place in Boston. She was acquitted but, it is said, was arrested and imprisoned again in 1675. Once more she was found not guilty. Returning to Springfield, Joseph became one of the most prosperous men in western Massachusetts. Benjamin also became an important citizen and Deacon of the Springfield Congregational Church.

Thomas Spratt

Thomas Spratt was probably born in Beaminster and he was certainly baptised in St Mary's Church in 1635. His first schooling was at 'a little church at the churchyard side'. He went up to Wadham College, Oxford, graduated and became a fellow in 1657. He was appointed Bishop of Rochester in 1684 and went on to become a man of influence. He lived in turbulent times and when William of Orange came to claim the throne it was Bishop Spratt who brought the royal crowns and administered the chalice at the

Thomas Spratt (1635–1713), Bishop of Rochester and Dean of Westminster.

coronation. He later read the sermon when William's successor Queen Anne was crowned in 1702. He was a founder member of the Royal Society.

John Seymour

Born in 1738, John Seymour was baptised at St Mary's Church. He had completed his apprenticeship as a joiner by 1759 and moved to Axminster where he had his own carpentry workshop and made furniture. In 1784 he emigrated to America and made his name as a cabinet maker. He is considered one of America's most prominent craftsmen of the period and a number of examples of his work are still in the White House.

Samuel Hearne

The renowned explorer Samuel Hearne once lived in Beaminster and his remarkable exploits are believed by many to be the inspiration for the character of the Eternal Wanderer in Samuel Taylor Coleridge's 1797 epic poem *The Rime of the Ancient Mariner*.

Hearne was four years old when his father died in 1750. His mother Diana returned to Beaminster where she had been born and Samuel attended Frances Tucker's Free School. He was not a good student, 'his dislike to reading and writing was so great that he made little progress in either' but he was rather fond of drawing. He became determined to follow in the footsteps of his hero Robinson Crusoe and go to sea. His mother knew the seafaring Hood family of Netherbury and Samuel was engaged to serve under Captain (later Admiral) Samuel Hood. He saw action against the French and gained rapid promotion in the Navy.

After he was discharged Hearne joined the Hudson Bay Company, arriving in Canada in 1766, and at the age of 24 was sent north to find copper for the company and to discover whether reports of a Northwest Passage were true. Two early attempts were aborted but in December 1770 he set out again with a Dene Indian guide. After nearly 18 months, during which Hearne witnessed the Dene Indians massacre 20 Inuit at Bloody Falls, his party reached the coast where the Far-Off Metal River met the sea and he erected the company's mark. Poor health forced his retirement from the Hudson Bay Company in 1787 and he settled in London. He died in 1792, aged 47.

Richard Waygood

Richard Waygood was born Beaminster in 1806 and started a business in the town in 1833. His general engineering works included the manufacture of stoves and hot-water apparatus. In 1842 he transferred his works to London and was joined by one of his foremen, John Marsh Day. His foundry flourished and in 1863 he and his nephew built the Newington Iron Works. By 1868 the company had received its first order for a hydraulic lift and about 90 years later the firm was taken over by Otis, the famous manufacturer of lifts and elevators.

Gertrude Bugler

Born in 1897 into a Dorchester family Gertrude Bugler had a passion for amateur dramatics and performed with the Dorchester Debating and Dramatic Society. Thomas Hardy adapted some of his stories for them and the group took the name The Hardy Players. He had seen Gertrude act in 1913 and when she played the part of Eustacia Vye in the Players' performance of *The Return of the Native* in

The Bugler family, c.1913, with Gertrude in the centre.

Gertrude Bugler in the centre of the front row with The Hardy Players, c.1920.

1920 Hardy described her 'tall and dark' appearance as exactly what he had in mind for the character.

In 1921 she married Captain Ernest Frank Bugler who, in 1918, had been awarded the Military Cross whist serving in Afghanistan, and came to live in Beaminster. The *Bridport News*, under the headline 'Famous Hardy Player Weds' described her thus:

The bride, who is extremely popular and is the leading lady in Mr Thomas Hardy's players, has gained much fame by her clever histrionic powers. It will be recalled that she received many tempting offers to appear on the London stage, all of which she has refused...

But in 1924 Hardy himself requested her to play the part of Tess in *Tess of the d'Urbervilles* in Dorchester. Hardy died in 1928 but she went on to take the leading role when the play was staged in London in 1929. After a long and successful run Gertrude Bugler returned to her ordinary life in Beaminster and never acted professionally again.

Names to Remember

There are many families who have left their mark on the town and whose names are almost synonymous with Beaminster. Many tradespeople are mentioned elsewhere in this book; others include John Banger Russell (1760–1827) who was Beaminster's first historian contributing to Hutchins' *History and Antiquities of the County of Dorset*; Thomas Hine (1775–1822), founder of the Hine cognac house in Jarnac, France; Samuel Symes Cox (1817–84) who was the first Chief Constable of Dorset; and Richard Hine (1860–1939) an expert photographer who published his *History of Beaminster* in 1914. In addition, the names of Cox, Kitson, Trotman, Russell and Leigh were synonymous with the legal profession in the town.

Beaminster doctors have been prominent in the history of the town. Early in the eighteenth century Henry Dunning at Bridge House was a Doctor of Physick, Dr James Dunning resided there in the late 1700s and Joachim Gilbert, a surgeon previously of

The wedding of Richard Hine and Mabel Holloway in 1897. Left to right, back row: Edward Smith, ?; front row: Dora Bowditch, Minnie Gillingham, Richard Hine, Mabel Hine née Holloway, ?, ?.

John Lane Kitson, solicitor, and his wife at their home, The Yews, c.1920. He was chairman of Beaminster Water Supply and Sewerage Committee in the early 1900s.

Dr Joachim Gilbert and his wife in the garden of Bridge House. Early 1920s.

Dr A.A. Pim with his wife Ethel Charlotte and their daughters, Kathleen ('Yummy') and Evelyn ('Sissy') at the rear of their home, The Walnuts, c.1912.

East Street, in the 1870s. John Daniel (d.1781) who was a 'celebrated surgeon of this town' lived at Prout Bridge; John Daniel (d.1829) was a doctor and his sons James William Daniel (d.1859) and Thomas Palmer Daniel (d.1853) were surgeons. Dr A.A. Pim had the first motorcar in Beaminster and Dr Herbert Lake, known as 'the doctor on horseback' for his preferred mode of transport and his love of hunting, led the Mounted Home Guard in the 1940s. Other medical practitioners whose names are well remembered also served the townspeople and village inhabitants.

Kathleen Charlotte Barclay Pim

Dr Pim's eldest daughter, Kathleen Charlotte Barclay Pim (1903–2000), nicknamed 'Yummy', was a favourite personality in the town where she spent most of her life. During her lifetime she witnessed many monumental events in the town's history. She saw the first car in Beaminster; the devastating influenza epidemic of 1918 which killed her father's partner Dr Kitson of whom she said, 'he was ill in the morning and he was dead in the evening'; she taught cookery in the late 1920s and during the Second World War she was a volunteer nurse with the Voluntary Aid Detachment at Stoke Water House. She was also conscripted into the testing laboratory at the milk factory. She taught in the Sunday School and was an enthusiastic member of the Beaminster Ramblers Association and later the Beaminster Amblers.

Miss Kathleen Pim, 1903–2000.

William Guppy

There were, of course, a host of ordinary people whose names may not have been recorded for posterity but whose faces were captured by the camera. One photographer was William Guppy, born in Beaminster in 1893. He started photography as a hobby, enlisted in the Royal Flying Corps as a photographer from 1914 to 1916 and after the war returned to Fleet Street in Beaminster to set up as a photographer from 1919 to 1930. Many of his portrait photographs have survived and although today we don't know who all the subjects were the images provide an evocative record of the period.

Cecil Poole

Another well-known Beaminsterian is Cecil Poole, who ran a building company in the town and was a bellringer at St Mary's Church for over 60 years. He celebrated his 103rd birthday in 2006.

Winnie Emery? c.1910.

Family group, c.1900–05.

Soldier and young woman, c.1914–18.

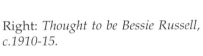

Right: *Thought to be Bessie Russell, c.1910-15.*

Far right: *Jack Newton who lived in Fleet Street, c.1900–20.*

Thought to be Lily White who may have worked at Pines, the grocers, c.1915–19.

Young woman, c.1915.

Thought to be Mrs Gunning with Edith, Bessie and Charlie, c.1905–10.

Above: *H.G. Russell, 1901–89.*

Above right: *Revd Alfred Codd, vicar of Beaminster, 1857–90.*

Right: *Revd Arthur A. Leonard, vicar of Beaminster for 12 years from 1890.*

Above: *J.R. Cox, 1905.*

Emily Hine, c.1868-70.

Col G.F. Pinney of Horn Park, 1912.

Rear view of the Tithe Barn at Corscombe Court, showing the moat.

Corscombe: 'The Ground Where Hollis Lies...'

Corscombe's roots lie far in the past. There are standing stones near Beckham's Coppice, possibly the remains of a Neolithic long barrow, and one of its stones is known locally as the Devil's Armchair. There is also a mysterious alignment of recumbent stones in Brackett's Lane. Up on Toller Down there are two large sarsen stones called the Hoar Stones. These are said to be boundary markers, perhaps of Saxon origin, but probably of a much earlier date. They are just off the A356 at the point where there is a turning on the left to Beaminster Down. The name Corscombe is thought to mean 'valley of the pass-road or pass-gate' from the Old English words *Cors Weg Cumb*. In either case, the pass in question is what is now known as Wynyards Gap.

There was certainly a Saxon settlement at Corscombe as evidenced from an early charter of AD754, whereby Corscombe was given to the Abbey Church of Sherborne (and it remained in the hands of the abbey until the Dissolution of the Monasteries in 1539). In 1014 Ethelred ('the Unready') confirmed an early charter which combined a brief history of the estate at Corscombe, mentioning that it consisted of one steep street halfway up an escarpment on the chalk hills ten miles southwest of Sherborne. These charters affirm three early land units. Corscombe itself was separate from Catsley, which in turn was separate from Benville (formerly Earnley). They were later all included in one parish.

In the Domesday Survey in 1086 the major part of the land was owned by the Bishop of Salisbury, and lesser amounts by William, Earl of Moriton and by Goodwin, one of the King's thanes.

Corscombe Court

Corscombe Court was originally a grange of

The Tithe Barn at Corscombe Court.

Sherborne Abbey and the abbot acted as lord of the manor. It was here that the abbots held the manor courts. The house dates back to the thirteenth century, though there was probably an earlier building on the site. The crossing at the south end was added c.1700. An interesting feature is the moat which virtually surrounds the house and barn. The owner claims it is the only working moat in Dorset, and certainly boat trips on the moat are always very popular at the annual Corscombe Fête. The Tithe Barn is of the fifteenth century.

After the abbey was dissolved Corscombe, together with Halstock and Netherstoke, was granted in 1551 to Richard Fermor. It remained with this family until 1741. A survey exists of these manors in 1684 and it is interesting to note that when Sir William Fermor leased his house at Corscombe to Sir Andrew Henley in 1653, special arrangements were made so that Sir William could still hold court twice a year every three years, and be provided with hospitality for himself and his men and horses, for seven days.

Religious and Civic Strife

Corscombe was not untouched by the religious turmoil of the sixteenth and seventeenth centuries. On the whole Beaminster and the surrounding villages were Protestant in their sympathies, but there were many who kept to the Roman Catholic religion and centres of this were known at Mapperton and Axnoller. Despite the fact that in the 1580s laws against Catholicism and its priests became much harsher, mass was celebrated in Corscombe in a house belonging to Whittle and it is known that William Coltleigh attended services there. A small shrine has been discovered in Epple Cottage, and it is possible that it may have been connected with secret masses at this time.

Benville Manor was owned by two Roman Catholic ladies, Winifred and Elizabeth Brereton and in 1626 the house was attacked by a company of Protestant soldiers from Evershot who demanded money. Fortunately for the two ladies they had been warned in advance by a neighbour and had managed to barricade the house and take refuge on the first floor. Terrified, they threw some gold coins to the soldiers who eventually left. There was probably a chapel in the house at this time, and masses celebrated, but no trace now remains.

Some of the men of Corscombe were involved in the Monmouth Rebellion. The Duke of Monmouth, son of Charles II, landed in Lyme Regis in 1685 and rallied many men of the West Country in support of his claim to the Crown, as there was dissatisfaction in the country at King James II's Catholic tendencies. Monmouth and his army were defeated at Sedgemoor and those supporting him were tried at Dorchester by Judge Jeffries in what became known as the Bloody Assize. Robert Fawn of Corscombe was hanged for his part and his body dismembered, boiled in pitch and publicly exhibited.

Smuggling

In the eighteenth century Corscombe, among many other villages in Dorset, was heavily involved in smuggling. The goods were landed on the coast and then moved inland to be later distributed further afield. Both Corscombe and Halstock are reputed to have had sites where smuggled goods were hidden. In Halstock it was Pear Tree Farm, and in Corscombe a cottage called Woodwalls. There was a school in this in the cottage with, it is said, large vaults beneath which the schoolboys had helped to dig to hide the contraband.

Population Shifts

In 1841 the population of Corscombe went up to 810, but thereafter declined until the figure had almost halved by 1901. Agricultural depression was one reason, but particularly in Corscombe and Halstock, it was due to emigration, as was mentioned in an official report. However, in 1851 the area was still thriving with 16 farmers and, among others, dairymen, carpenters, blacksmiths, a stonemason, a tailor, a dressmaker and milliner, a miller and baker, a butcher, a grocer and draper, and a publican. The 1851 census also mentions that a family of gypsies, Thomas and Harriet James, their son, Thomas, his wife Mary and their nine children aged between one and 16, were living in the village. 'Travellers' are not a new phenomenon!

Education in Corscombe

Although a school building was erected in 1872 following the 1870 Education Act, Corscombe had its own village school 30 years earlier, when a building was erected on the church glebe for the education of poor children. The 1872 building became Corscombe National School and continued until 1964 when it was closed due to

Corscombe School c.1932. Left to right, back row, standing on floor: *?, George Hawkins, Fred Diment;* standing on bench: *Tom Watts, Basil Davis, ?;* standing on floor: *Cyril Mintern, ?, ?, ?;* on rocking horse: *Bertie Cornish, Kenneth Mintern;* middle row: *Miss Gould, ?, Kathleen Childs, ?, Marjorie Banwell, ?, Millie Holloway;* sitting: *?, Lily Gale, ?, Gertie Wrixon, Sybil Davis, ?, Dolly Gale;* front row, kneeling: *?;* sitting: *Harold Diment, Stanley Holloway.*

falling attendance. The building was bought by the parishioners and has become the Village Hall, replacing the old hall which was affectionately known as The Hut.

Corscombe Church

Corscombe Church originally had two dedications, St Mary and St Michael, but is now solely dedicated to St Mary the Virgin. There must have been a church here from early in the fourteenth century as the list of rectors goes back to 1315, but it was completely rebuilt in the fifteenth century, with the tower and the north porch dating from this rebuilding. In 1746 the condition of the church was poor and it was extensively repaired and part of the chancel rebuilt at the expense of Thomas Hollis (of whom more below). At this time the gallery was extended across the whole of the west end. Over a century later the church was again found to be in a state of decay and a further reconstruction was carried out. Some of the eighteenth-century work was swept away, including the gallery which was then considered ugly. The final cost of this work was £2,373.18s.7d. The architect was Mr Allen of Crewkerne.

St Mary's Church, Corscombe.

Corscombe church and old rectory, now Corscombe House.

Benville

Benville is also included in the parish of Corscombe. According to the Dorset historian

Hutchins, 'it anciently belonged to the Kymers, Lords of West Chelborough, at whose court tenants of Benville were obliged to do suit and service.' It has a fine manor house, probably built in the early-seventeenth century. Its previous name was Earnley, which in 1086 was part of the estate of Frampton Priory. Possibly the new name of Benville came from the family of John de Benefeld who lived in this area in 1340. He may have lived in the earlier manor house which no longer exists. Benville was bought in 1620 by Winifred and Elizabeth Brereton, whose story is outlined above. Winifred married George Arundell of Netherbury and the property remained in the hands of their Roman Catholic descendants for about 200 years.

Buildings of Character

There are many old buildings in Corscombe, such as Court Farm, which is reputed to be one of the oldest houses in Dorset; the Fox Inn; Corscombe House next to the church and originally the rectory; High Orchards; Pope's Cottage; Lilac Cottage and Lower Farm. The size of the village has varied greatly over the years and although it has lost its school, shop and Post Office it continues to develop and flourish – and still retains its well-known pub!

Toller Whelme

Not far away lies Toller Whelme hamlet whose name refers to the source of the River Toller (Toller is the old name of the River Hooke). The hamlet was a grange of Forde Abbey until the Dissolution of the Monasteries. It is said that the Race Ground field at Pipsford was used in medieval times when spectators were encouraged to bet on the horse races. The manor house includes elements dating from the fifteenth, seventeenth and eighteenth centuries. An early part of the building was always known as the Chapel. The manor was sold to the Pennes of East Coker and Chedington in 1630. George Penne was a keen Royalist and after the Civil War, because of his loyalty to the King, he sustained heavy expense, sequestration and debt.

In 1802 Toller Whelme was bought by the Pope family and in 1869 William Pope built St John's Church there consisting of a chancel, nave and small tower. At this time there was a population of 100 in the hamlet.

To mark the end of the First World War the airships that had been based at Hooke Park and patrolled the Channel, flew over Toller Whelme, Toller Down and Beaminster with large Union Flags on their sides. The aeronautical theme continued when, in about 1921/2, there was an air rally at Toller Whelme which saw small aircraft, including biplanes with canvas skins on a wooden frame, ex-World-War-One aircraft and some monoplanes, compete for prizes. Well-known fliers of the day such as the Duchess of Bedford and Amy Johnson attended. One eyewitness remembered that 'the spectators tended to poke holes in the canvas' which were 'mended with patches and off flew the aircraft'! There was even a bombing raid over Parnham with mock bombs.

Toller Whelme has always been a quiet hamlet, and even in 1947 Aubrey de Selincourt could write, 'one might live in Dorset forever and not even know it is there.'

Thomas Hollis (1720–74)

Both Corscombe and Halstock have some very unusual field names and they owe these to Thomas Hollis of Essex who, in 1749, purchased a large acreage of land in the two villages. After all, where else do you find fields called Cassius, Brutus or Messala, Toleration or Education, Massachusetts or Boston?

Hollis was born in 1720 and was given the liberal education considered suitable for one who was to be heir to a large fortune. According to Hutchins, the Dorset historian, 'He early acquired that ardent love of liberty and freedom of sentiment which strongly marked his character.' He travelled widely in Europe and on his return wished to enter Parliament but, horrified by the bribery which this entailed at the time, he abandoned the idea. Instead he turned his attention to his collection of books and medals, and

... to the purpose of illustrating and upholding liberty, preserving the memory of its champions, to render tyranny and its abettors odious and to extend science and art.

He became a benefactor on a grand scale and made gifts of many collections of books to libraries in Europe. He also made many benefactions yearly to Harvard University in America, beginning in 1758. The town of Holliston is named after him and there is a Hollis Hall at Harvard University. He arranged to have republished numerous books and treatises by authors of whom he approved and, importantly to us in Dorset, encouraged Hutchins to write his monumental *History* of this county.

In 1741 he bought his estates in Corscombe and Halstock, but did not fulfil his desire to move down here until 1770 when he came to live at Urles Farm, Corscombe, where he resided until his death in 1774.

Hollis seems to have been a conscientious landlord and did much to restore the local churches, although he himself was a dissenter – some even said he was an atheist. He was regarded by his contemporaries as an eccentric and some of his political views were termed 'democratical', which was no recommendation at that time. He was not popular with the establishment as can be imagined, believing as he did in the principle of political liberty. He was an odd character, interesting, independent of mind but a practical philanthropist and in a true sense public spirited.

His legacy to Corscombe and Halstock was his renaming of the farms and their fields which he had purchased from the Fermor family in 1740. He called them by the names of the champions of liberty for the most part, this being interpreted as anyone who had helped free the human spirit. Neville, Locke, Sydney, Marvell, Harrington and Milton Farms are named after authors of whom he approved; Harvard Farm after the American university and Liberty Farm which is self-explanatory. Renaming the farms would have been enough for most people, but Hollis was not content until he had renamed most of the fields as well. Some were again called after patriots and heroes whom he venerated, some after abstract virtues, some after American states. Here is a sample of the names he gave: Lycurgus, Solon, Socrates, Pythagoras, Cicero, Pelopidas, Timoleon, Education, Constitution, Toleration, Understanding, Reasonableness, Boston, Cotton, Massachusetts, William III, Stuart Coppice, Free State, Commonwealth, Pym, Leighton, Hampden, Lilburne, Berne, Geneva, Bradshaw, Ireton, Reformation, Cromwell, Henry VIII, Knox, Bacon, Vaughan, Seldon, Luther, Calvin, Coligny, Wycliff, Magna Carta. If you are wondering why Stuart Coppice is included, the answer is that the hazel trees had to be beheaded often!

What did the inhabitants of Corscombe think of these sometimes outlandish and hard-to-pronounce names? Did they ignore them at first and stick to the more familiar 'cowleaze' or 'furzy ground'? It must surely have taken some time for them to be accepted. Nevertheless, when the tithe maps were produced in 1841 most of the Hollis names were still there and what is more they are still in use today! A lasting legacy indeed.

A verse in Crowe's poem *Lewesdon Hill* pays a graceful tribute to Hollis:

Fair would I view thee, Corscombe, fain would hail
The ground where Hollis lies; his choice retreat
Where from the busy world withdrawn, he lived,
To generous virtue, and the holy love
Of liberty, a dedicated spirit;
And left his ashes there; still honouring
Thy fields with title given of patriotic names,
But more with his untitled sepulchre.

Kimberley Cottage on the road to Halstock, with part of the roof still thatched.

Pitts Farm. Once a pub called the George Inn, it later became a bakery, then reverted back to a farm.

Interior of the lime-kiln at Hill Farm. It has a pointed draw arch, typical of the area around Corscombe.

Corscombe WI's production of Much Ado About Nothing, *at Benville Manor, 1928. Left to right, back row: Leonato – Mrs Barrett, Benedick – Miss Protheroe, Claudio – Ethel Wareham, The Prince – Mrs Troyte-Bullock (producer); sitting: Margaret – Miss Goodchild, Beatrice – Miss Elaine Storrs, Hero – Grace Bath, Ursula – Nurse Hawkins; front row: Musician – Marjorie Morey, Musician – Nancy Holloway, Balthazar – Doris Bath.*

Above: *St Mary's Cottage.*

Above: *Corscombe Post Office when it was at St Mary's Cottage.*

Above: *Corscombe Post Office, when it was at High Orchards.*

Left: *Particulars of the Corscombe Model Steam Bakery, 1920.*

LOT 6.

(Coloured Yellow on enlarged Plan.)

THE WELL-PLACED AND COMPLETELY EQUIPPED

Business Premises

KNOWN AS

The Corscombe Model Steam Bakery,

comprising a

Double-fronted Dwelling-house

substantially erected of stone with slated roof, containing :—Sitting Room, Kitchen with Range, Larder, Back Kitchen with Grate, 4 Good Bedrooms (1 with Grate), Landing and Stairs. Outside E.C.

THE BUSINESS PREMISES

are stone-built and slated, and comprise :—Fitted shop communicating with the house, Bakehouse and Stokehole, Coal Store, Wash-house with Furnace, Waggon House, 2 Piggeries and Stable with loft over.

EXCELLENT WATER SUPPLY laid on from the Spring on Lot 5 to a Stand-pipe near the back door.

Small Flower Garden and Large Productive Kitchen Garden.

TWO VERY HEALTHY MEADOWS with water supply available.

The whole of these centrally situated and conveniently arranged premises extends to an area of

1 A.   2 R.   37 P.

as shewn in the following Schedule :—

No. on Plan.	Name.	Description.	A.	R.	P.
11	The Corscombe Bakery ...	... Buildings, etc. ...	... 0	1	15
540	Home Ground ...	... Meadow ...	... 0	2	18
Pt. 541	Little Plot ...	... ditto...	... 0	3	4
			A. 1	**2**	**37**

Let to Mr. W. J. Barge with other lands at an apportioned rental of £20 per annum.

The Tenant has agreed to give up possession on 29th September, 1920, in accordance with the special arrangements mentioned in the General Remarks.

Tithe, Commuted Value, 13s. 3d.   Land Tax, 17s. 0d.

The following fixtures are claimed by the Tenant :—Counter and fittings in Shop, Glazed door to Cupboard, Baking Oven and fittings in Bakehouse, Supply Piping from Standpipe to Oven, Galvanized Iron Trap House, Stabling, Chaff House, Open Shed, and Harness House in yard.

Chapter 3
Of Fire and Flood

Narrow streets crowded with old timbered buildings and roofs of thatch made many of the towns in Dorset a high fire risk, and Beaminster was no exception. There were two extensive fires in the seventeenth century. It was Palm Sunday, 14 April 1644 when a fire began. The Civil War was in progress and Prince Maurice and the Royalist army were quartered in the town. This was bitterly resented by the inhabitants whose sympathies lay with the Parliamentarians. In addition there was quarrelling among the Royalist troops, and the Beaminster historian Richard Hine suggests that in view of the general unrest Prince Maurice gave orders to fire the town. On the other hand, a broadside published in 1684 refers to the loyalty of Beaminster inhabitants to the King, and puts the blame for the fire on Cromwell's army! Whichever version you believe, the account of the fire itself runs as follows:

The fire was first kindled in John Sargeant's house in Northe Streete and it was a musket discharged in the Gable, and it was Wild Fire and the Wind being directly with the Towne, So that the whole Towne was all destroyed in two hours; and those goods for the most part which were carried out of the fire, were carried away by the Souldiers.

Not quite all the town was destroyed, East Street and part of Church Street were saved, but the devastation was immense. It must have been a bleak Easter in 1644.

In the following year the Parliamentary army was at Beaminster and the Parliamentary chronicler, Joshua Spriggs, recorded that it was 'a place of the pityfulest spectacle that man can behold, hardly a house left not consumed by fire.' In all 144 houses were destroyed at an estimated value of £21,080. The people of Beaminster applied to Parliament for help, and obtained an order raising £2,000 out of the confiscated estates of a prominent local Royalist, George Penny of Toller Whelme. The actual money was very slow in coming. By January 1648 only £800 (£300 in money and £500 in timber trees) had been provided. The remaining £1,200 would only begin to be paid off in three years' time, and then only at the rate of £100 a year.

As if this were not enough misfortune, there was another devastating fire in June 1684, just as the town was beginning to get back on its feet. It is not known how and when it started, but the areas affected seem to have been the north and central parts of the market-place (the Square) and the north side of Hogshill Street and East Street (Prout Hill). Buildings affected included the Town Hall and the Shambles, and the White Hart. The Market House and the Shambles were extensively damaged as was the house of Frances Tucker, heiress of William Tucker, which had relatively recently been built in the Square. It was a good stone house, three storeys high, with three rooms on each floor. Only finished in 1673, she lived in the house for but a brief period. Her claim for it was £500, the highest amount for a private house. On the north side of the Square at the corner of Fleet Street and North Street was a house which bears a unique record of the 1684 fire.

A total of £13,684 was claimed, which included property and goods, and an official Parliamentary Brief was issued so that monies could be collected from every part of England. Contributions are in fact recorded from places such as Mere in Wiltshire and Ormsby St Margaret in Norfolk. It must have taken a long time for the town to recover from these two fires. However, as Richard Hine put it:

Phoenix like, once more Beaminster rose from its ashes; this time with wider streets and substantial stone houses many of which yet remain.

Almost a hundred years passed before there was another serious fire in Beaminster. It was recorded in 1781 that:

Between the hours of 4 and 5 in the morning, a Fire broke out in a back building belonging to the Kings

The plaque on No. 12 the Square, now barely legible.

Arms Inn... In the course of Three or Four Hours all the Houses on the West side of the street leading from the Market Place to the church (only two excepted) were destroyed. At the same time, Two houses near the Pound, with the School House, and several houses near the Alms House, together with all the houses in Church Street and Schederick Street... and Eight houses on the South side of Hogshill Street, besides stables and other buildings, were entirely consumed. The whole number of Houses destroyed amounted to upwards of fifty.

On this occasion a greater part of people's goods were saved, but sadly Betty, the daughter of the schoolmaster William Pavy, was burnt to death.

At the time of the two great fires in the seventeenth century the only available equipment to fight fires was buckets of water drawn from rivers or wells, and probably hand squirts or syringes. Gradually manual fire-engines began to be manufactured, and the first one in Beaminster was bought in 1712 by public subscription. Further engines were purchased later in the century and a large reservoir constructed under the roadway in the market-place to ensure a plentiful supply of water. Eventually more sophisticated fire appliances were introduced, in the nineteenth and twentieth centuries, and today Beaminster has a fire station and a retained fire crew to deal with fires and floods.

The early-nineteenth-century fire pump.

Major floods have occurred several times in Beaminster including those recorded on 16 October 1876, 25 August 1894, 23 October 1961 and in 1979. J.B. Russell recorded for 16 October 1786, 'a very high flood, the oldest people do not remember greater.' The most disastrous flood occurred during the night of 25-26 August 1894. Rain had been falling for several days and culminated in a severe thunderstorm, which broke over the town shortly before midnight. The *Bridport News* published an extensive report describing the disaster:

Never has Beaminster had such a terrible visitation in the shape of a flood as on Saturday night and Sunday morning and it will be remembered with terror by

many to the end of their days... Torrents of water poured down the surrounding hills into the town, and the experience of many of the inhabitants was described as a night of terror. Garden walls were thrown down, bridges swept away houses partially wrecked, their contents being washed down the river to Netherbury.

The garden wall of Mr Hardcastle's house, Woodlands, was 'a solid piece of masonry two feet thick, and in Southgate is 12ft. high' but at about a quarter to midnight:

... Mr Grimes noticed water flowing over this high wall opposite his house. The wall suddenly gave way, a clean breach being made a length of fully 50 feet, and the force of the water was such that that it also knocked over the wall on the show field side, making an opening of about the same extent. The wonder is that the cottages opposite were not also swept away, and probably would have been but for the vent the torrent found through Mr Hunt's shop and timber yard, through Mr Grimes's house, and through a pair of large doors a little higher up in the same row, which were knocked to pieces and carried away by the flood.

Mr Grimes and Mr Hunt were trapped in the downstairs rooms of their adjoining cottages with the water level almost reaching the ceiling whilst their families were trapped upstairs. The two families broke down the wooden partitions between the cottages and joined each other on Mr Hunt's side. Meanwhile Mr Hunt had torn down some of the ceiling and told the women to take up the floorboards. They used every implement available and broke them all, eventually wrenching up the floorboards with their bare hands and allowing Mr Hunt to squeeze through. Realising that Mr Grimes was still trapped they succeeded in getting him out half conscious using a long lath from a bedstead for him to grab.

The newspaper reporter viewed the damage at Captain Russell's house, Beridth, for himself:

I expressed amazement when I saw the high massive wall, built with large blocks of stone, lying in the street demolished as though there had been an Alexandrian bombardment at Beaminster... There is no wall between the lawn and the garden but the boundary wall on the far side is laid as flat on the ground as you would lay a book on a table... and you may walk upon it as you would a paved floor... Another curious thing is that each of the flower stands in the porch was turned upside down. The water struck the library window... entered the library, and turned everything over. The water mark in this room is shown at 5 feet 10 inches, and as a piano stood there one need hardly suggest that much will have to be done before exquisite touch and tone are restored. In every room of the house, however, an immense amount of damage has been done, and

Above: *Southgate showing the 12-foot-high wall that collapsed after water came over the top. The cottages opposite are where Mr Hunt and Mr Grimes were trapped in the ground floor rooms with only little air left near the ceiling and from which they both made dramatic escapes.*

Right: *Damage to the wall near to Bridge House showing the debris in Captain Russell's garden. The policeman is presumably protecting the entry to the garden from sightseers or looters.*

Captain Russell was right in saying the demolition of the outer walls was nothing as compared with the ruinous state of things in the house and grounds.

The local police were also involved.

Damage to the wall between Captain Russell's garden and the road with Bridge House in the background.

Of course the police-station itself, and yard, were flooded as well as the houses just below. The water in the street at this point reached close up to the bedroom window of one of the houses, and here PC Pearce showed himself. Divesting himself of boots and tunic, he swam from the bank to the lamp post in very deep water, at the time when all was darkness and the roaring waters were sufficient to shake the nerves of most people. His intention was to light the lamp, but he failed owing to no gas being turned on. For this purpose he swam to one of the bedroom windows, and a woman seeing a man in the water shouted: 'Oh! a man's

Extensive damage to the properties opposite the collapsed wall by Captain Russell's garden. The houses were so badly damaged that they had to be demolished. New houses, some of brick, were built in their place.

Prout Bridge carriage works, when the damaged carriages had been removed, showing the extent of the damage. Mr Hann of Prout Bridge lost a 40 gallon drum of oil in the flood.

in the water and will be drowned.' Pearce, however, coolly said he was 'only a policeman' and would take no harm, but would she give him a candle to light the lamp! She did so, and I say – well done Pearce!

Further down the river there was considerable debris at the weir at Clenham. One of Captain Russell's big doors was found there as well as a heavy lathe wheel and frame from Mr Hunt's workshop. One Beaminster boy, a rabbit fancier, lost his entire stock-in-trade of Belgian hares, Himalayas, Angoras and Dutch, with their hutches, which were carried away to Netherbury.

Local photographer Richard Hine sold photographic views of the disaster at 9d. and 1s. each, some of which are shown in this chapter.

Over half a century later, in November 1960, Benjamin Pond recorded visiting his brother-in-law, Norman Dore, the police sergeant who lived at the old Beaminster police station:

Clenham weir with large pieces of wood that were reported to have come from Captain Russell's house in the middle of Beaminster.

Flooding in Hogshill Street with the fire brigade in attendance, 1979.

Above left: *Norman Welsford observing the 1979 flood.*

Above: *The fire brigade in action, 1979.*

Left: *The dam above Gerrards Green was built to prevent flooding of the estate and restrict the rise of the River Brit in Beaminster. The stream goes through the sluice in the middle centre of the picture. To the right is the reservoir storage area. When the water level rises in the stream there is a secondary storage area to the right of the picture.*

The bridge by the Red House in North Street completely demolished. The stream coming in here would be one of those that flooded into Southgate by the road when the channel overflowed.

... I saw a surging mass of water rushing by; across the road on the opposite side was a milk factory and churns were being carried away in the flood; soon a police car and a van outside were likewise swept on down the road; then came some beer and great bulks of timber...

This flood was apparently caused by a combination of a cloud burst on the surrounding hills, the river bursting its banks and a fractured water main.

The following year the fire station log at Beaminster recorded the flood of 23 October 1961:

... at 9.35p.m. Station Officer Park was asked to inves-

tigate flooding. By 9.42a.m. appliance had been sent to Southgate and an emergency water pump (a Green Goddess) was parked in East Street. The appliance from Maiden Newton had been sent to Hooke and then on to Southgate. By 10p.m. the Halstock appliance was also called to Beaminster. By 2 a.m. the following morning the Halstock appliance had been stood down and the Beaminster appliances returned to the station at 4 a.m.

After the flood of 1979 a flood protection scheme was built which included a dam above Gerrards Green. This seems to have prevented further severe flooding.

The damage in the mill grounds was caused by the several streams that all joined the River Brit. The miller, William Curtis, and the next door tenant, John Shepherd, were trapped upstairs in the mill. Four feet of water had found its way into the mill and 200 sacks of corn were damaged, but fortunately there were none in the basement.

Halstock: Mosaics and Martyrdom

The name Halstock means 'holy place', and it is thought this name refers to the small community of monks who were living here in Saxon times, as mentioned in a charter of AD847. Others think it may refer to St Juthware, a local saint, who is believed to have been martyred here. The story of Halstock begins a good deal earlier as there is known to have been a flourishing Iron Age settlement here on the site of the Roman villa which later replaced it. Older still is the Neolithic trackway, the Harrow Way, which goes through the centre of the village and on through Corscombe to Beaminster Down where it meets the Great Ridgeway.

The Iron Age settlement dates from the first century BC and seems to have lasted until the middle of the first century AD. It was followed in the second century AD by the Roman villa. This went through various modifications over a period of time, finally becoming a courtyard-type villa by the late-third century, and it is to this period that the fine mosaic floors date. These are geometric in design and belong to the Corinian school of mosaicists, who were based in Cirencester. The villa also possessed an elaborate bath suite which included a plunge pool, but some of the other domestic arrangements are unclear. The villa continued in use until at least AD400.

There is no evidence of sudden destruction, though no doubt it was used as a quarry for succeeding generations. It was rediscovered in the early 1800s when a mosaic floor was uncovered at the behest of the Earl of Ilchester, who then owned the land. Unfortunately, the villagers, convinced that treasure lay beneath, dug right through it at night hoping to find gold. What was left was then re-covered until excavations began in the 1960s.

Halstock has its own saint and for many years the village had a pub called The Quiet Woman with an inn sign showing her with her severed head under her arm. This image referred to the story of St Juthware or Judith who is said to have been martyred on a hill to the north of Halstock village. Her date is uncertain, but she probably lived around AD700.

Saint Juthware, A Martyr

Juthware was said to have been of noble British lineage, and from early years devoted herself to holy works. After her mother died, she remained in her father's house, attending to the needs of the visiting pilgrims there. She had a brother, Bana, and three sisters, Sidwella, Wilgitha and Edwara, who also later became saints. Her father remarried, and the new stepmother, who was jealous of Juthware's piety, tried to cause trouble. Her opportunity came after Juthware's father died. Juthware, who looked pale and ill as a result of much fasting and keeping vigil, complained of pains in her chest. Her stepmother, pretending maternal affection, advised her to apply freshly made cheese to her chest before going to church, assuring her that this would ease the pain.

Meanwhile the stepmother lied to Bana that Juthware was with child. Bana was a man quick to anger and ready to avenge misdeeds. When they came out of church, Bana accused Juthware of being pregnant, and finding her undergarments to be wet with milk, flew into a rage. Notwithstanding her denials, he struck off Juthware's head. It is said that she picked up her own head from the ground, and walked with it to the church where she placed it on the altar, watched in wonder by the gathered assembly. A

The Quiet Woman inn sign.

holy spring is said to have appeared in the place where her head fell, and certainly there is a vigorous spring today on the hill just next to the field which is called Judith. Needless to say, many miracles were said to have taken place there.

There is a local legend that Juthware's ghost haunts the scene of her martyrdom, but when one rector of Halstock, the Revd J. Slater, spent a night ghost hunting on the hill there was nothing to be seen. Later her relics were taken to Sherborne Abbey, and placed in a splendid tomb, and many more miracles were recorded. She became a very important saint there, and her feast day is recorded in the Sherborne Missal. In Beaminster Church there was a chantry chapel dedicated to St Mary and St Juthware, and her cult spread widely.

Early Halstock

There was a Saxon charter for Halstock, dating to 847 in which Ethelwulf, King of the Saxons, granted land here to Sherborne Abbey. The boundaries of the charter are easily followed on the ground today, as it reflects the current parish boundary, with the exception of the inclusion of the parish of Closworth, which is now in the county of Somerset. This must, therefore, represent a land-unit already in existence 1,100 years ago, and which may indeed be much older.

The Abbot's Court should have met in Halstock twice a year, but there is mention in the Court documents that very often this was reduced to once a year due to the appalling condition of the roads in bad weather! One can only sympathise.

After the Dissolution of the Monasteries Halstock, like Corscombe, was granted to Richard Fermor, and remained in the hands of this family until 1741 when it was purchased by Thomas Hollis who renamed many of the farms and fields here. More about Hollis is recorded in the section on Corscombe. Whilst a fascinating study in itself, this renaming has made it very difficult to trace farms and holdings before 1741. However, a survey of Corscombe and Halstock made in 1689 does suggest that landholding was still very fragmented, with many people holding small parcels of land within one small field. This may be a relic of an open field system of which there is very little other evidence locally. On the whole the parish seems to have been early enclosed.

St Mary's, Halstock

The church is dedicated to St Mary. The earliest part is the fifteenth-century tower, but there was almost certainly an earlier church on the site. In 1770 the nave and chancel were rebuilt following a fire. In 1845, because the roof was in poor condition, the decision was taken to rebuild the nave

and also to add a north aisle. The alterations were based on plans by A. Pugin, although not all his elaborate designs were followed. There are five bells in the tower of which four are by the Purdue family, bell-founders of Closworth. They were repaired and one recast in the 1960s by John Taylor of Loughborough, and rehung in 1967.

A Lunatic Asylum

Halstock was the home of one of the three private lunatic asylums in Dorset in the eighteenth century. It is first mentioned in 1722 when Edward Symes was paid for keeping a lunatic from Lyme Regis. It seems that Thomas Mercer took over after Symes' death, as he is mentioned as proprietor of a lunatic asylum in 1774. The premises were at Portland Farm. The Mercers were medical men through several generations and they continued to run the asylum until it was eventually closed in 1858, when provision was taken over by the County.

On the whole the asylum seems to have been well run and received favourable reports from the inspectors. At first there were four inmates, all from Somerset and Dorset, but this later increased to 30, with some from much farther afield.

A Changing Population

The population in Halstock reached a peak in 1841 with 626 inhabitants, but thereafter declined sharply, as did the populations of nearby Corscombe and Melbury. An official return suggests that this change was attributable to emigration. Many from Dorset went to North America, but one of those from Halstock went to Australia. This was William Hunt who emigrated in 1865 and settled near Sydney. His letter to the rector is mentioned in the parish magazine of 1905.

Schooling in Halstock

There was no school in Halstock until a grant was obtained in 1838 from the National Society for the Education of the Poor and a schoolroom was duly built. Foster's 1870 Education Act necessitated the enlargement of the school, and it was considerably extended, but at this stage did not yet include the small schoolroom and kitchen which were added in 1904/5.

The school flourished, but by 1986 the numbers were declining and it was closed. It was much missed by the village, the more so as the building had also been used as a Village Hall. However, necessity forced the inhabitants to act and a large new Village Hall was built in 1987.

The school log-book notes that more than once lessons had to be abandoned during the Second

Schoolchildren at Halstock, pre-1914.

World War on account of the noise caused by enemy aircraft overhead, added to, no doubt, by the anti-aircraft battery situated in Yeovil Showground. Several bombs were dropped in the vicinity, including three large ones in a field at East Chelborough. The body of a German airman was found by the stream at Springfield Farm. It was suggested that dropping through a clear sky, he was met by a thick mist such as is often seen in this valley, and assumed he had met the sea. He therefore released his parachute harness and fell to his death.

Development and Progress

Electricity did not arrive in the village until the late 1940s and mains water was not in use until the late 1950s, both making a vast difference to village life. The employment of the reservoir at Sutton Bingham from 1952 altered the Netherstoke end of the village, but created a splendid local amenity.

The original village shop in the Square closed in 1991, but a determined effort was made by the village and a Community Shop was set up in Spar Lodge. It continued there while plans for new premises were drawn up, and the purpose-built shop and Community Room were opened in 2001. The village lost its well-known pub The Quiet Woman and its loss is still mourned. However, Halstock still has a church, a shop and Post Office, a Community Room, a Village Hall and a golf club with restaurant, and remains a vibrant community.

The Square, c.1903, showing the shop in the background.

Halstock, looking towards the Square. Bethel House is on the right, a purpose-built chapel of unknown denomination.

Halstock House, c.1910. John Pring is on the left behind the hedge, while Sarah, his sister, is in front with the dog.

Celebration at Russell House, 7 July 1922, for the silver wedding of Richard and Mabel Hine. Their wedding photograph can be seen in Chapter 2.

The New Inn c.1900. The licensee at this time was William Hann.

Thatching the ridge at Liberty Farm.

Tree planting by the church to commemorate the closure of the school at Halstock in 1986. Seen here are the Bishop of Sherborne, John Kirkham and the Revd Gareth Miller.

Daniel's House. This part of the house was built after the 1781 fire.

On the left is Myrtle Cottage, built around 1800 and extended in the early-nineteenth century.

Chapter 4

Handsome Stone Houses of Beaminster

It is clear from documentary evidence that there was a Saxon minster in Beaminster and that it was in the ownership of Sherborne Abbey. During this early period the town seems to have been a small but thriving place. Its later prosperity is indicated by the rebuilding of the church in the thirteenth century. The development of the cloth industry must have helped to finance this rebuilding as well as the construction of the splendid tower. It has been suggested that East Street represents a planned extension of over 60 houses, each standing on a distinctive long plot which are unlike the more random arrangements in the rest of the town.

The historic buildings are mainly constructed with local yellow-brown Inferior Oolite limestone with Ham Hill limestone used for the important architectural details that had to be finely cut. Local Fuller's Earth clay has been used for good quality dark red and brown bricks and clay roofing tiles. Local building traditions have given a notable quantity and quality of details including canted bay windows, sashes and casements, grand doorcases with columns and pilasters and humbler bracketed canopies. There is also attractive ironwork to be seen in railings, fences, brackets, verandas and balconies.

In 1620 the Market House in the Square was rebuilt, and the chantry priest's house in the churchyard was replaced by an almshouse, now known as the Strode Room. The two disastrous fires in 1644 and 1684 (outlined in Chapter 3), which devastated large parts of the town, account for the general lack of pre-Georgian houses around the Square, and the survival of groups of older houses on the edge of the town. There are, however, some seventeenth-century buildings near the centre of the town. No. 12 the Square, on the corner of North Street and Fleet Street, was rebuilt in 1687 following the fire of 1684. Others are No. 5 Church Street, until recently the Eight Bells, and No. 56 Hogshill Street which has a large Tudor arch fireplace on the ground floor. Nos 19 and 21 North Street date from the mid-seventeenth century, and on the outskirts of town there are several exceptionally fine seventeenth-century houses which escaped the fires. Another serious fire followed in 1781 with further damage to property but in spite of these disasters the town survived. Most of the buildings in the Square are eighteenth and nineteenth century, some containing substantial remains of earlier periods, for example the HSBC Bank and the Greyhound.

Some buildings, worthy of mention, are outlined below. No. 19 Hogshill Street, formerly Devonia, has walls of ashlar and brick and was built in 1783 by Jeremiah Whitaker Newman, a surgeon, on the site of houses burnt in the fire of 1781. It was in the possession of the Hine family until 1886. No. 29 Hogshill Street, now called Daniel's House, was once owned by J.W. Daniel, also a surgeon. Its rear wing in Shadrack Street dates from the early-eighteenth century, while the front range in Hogshill Street is of a later date, replacing a building burnt in the 1781 fire. The Lodge on Tunnel Road, previously known as Beaminster House, was the home of Mary Clarke in 1830, who owned Meerhay Farm. Nearby is Myrtle Cottage once owned by James Rendle, a veterinary surgeon. It was built c.1800 and extended in the early-nineteenth century.

Champions in Hogshill Street was built in the late-seventeenth century and refaced in the nineteenth century. It has an ashlar stone façade. Built by Silas Symes, an attorney, it passed to the Russell family, and was lived in at one time by John Banger Russell, a Beaminster historian. Previously known as The Elms it was called Champions by Claud Streatfield, whose middle name was Champion. No. 52 Fleet Street, built c.1700, was once occupied by John and Richard Read who were wool-staplers. Barton End, at No. 50 Fleet Street, has a seventeenth-century stone house at the rear, and a front block of about 1730. It was owned in 1775 by Henry Willmott, wool-stapler.

Champions, once known as The Elms.

Above: *Bridge House dates from the early-seventeenth century. It is reputed to have a priest hole.*

Left: *Barton End, No. 50 Fleet Street.*

Below: *The Manor House, Beaminster.*

Hitts House, No. 14 Whitcombe Road. The door has a wooden shell-hood with a carved scallop shell. The gate piers with ball finials are eighteenth century.

The Walnuts. The front part was built c.1820. The rear part was built for Dr Pim in 1919.

Later it was occupied by Elizabeth Nicholls, who ran an academy for young ladies in the 1840s. From 1882 to 1897 it was used as premises for the Beaminster & Netherbury Grammar School. The Red House in North Street is an early-eighteenth century stone house, with a brick front in Flemish bond. It belonged to the Harris family, maltsters, and once had a malt-house attached on the rear.

Beaminster Manor House was once owned by Samuel Cox who acquired the property in 1767. The stables adjoining the house have been dated to c.1670 and were probably built by John Hoskins or his daughter, Mary Gifford. The house itself is of late-eighteenth-century construction, remodelled in the early nineteenth. A Tudor gateway from Clifton Maybank was erected in the garden and an ornamental lake made. In 1793 the garden and pleasure grounds were highly thought of by contemporaries.

Bridge House is a large, early-seventeenth-century house with stone mullions. Parts of the building may be even older. It was acquired early in the eighteenth century by Henry Dunning, a doctor, and later in the century by Dr James Dunning. Another doctor, Richard Phelps, in 1824 continued the medical link, later followed by Joachim Gilbert, surgeon. These premises are now the Bridge House Hotel. Farrs in Whitcombe Road is L-shaped, with a seventeenth-century rear part and an early-eighteenth century south range at right angles, with ashlar stone walls. It was known as Farrs in 1809, and seems to have been occupied by a Robert Farr in the late-seventeenth century.

Hitts House in Whitcombe Road, once owned by Phillis Dunning, dates from the late-seventeenth century, but was remodelled in the nineteenth. Presumably it was inherited from the Hitt family who built it. The marriage of Thomas Hitt to Mary

Dunning is recorded in 1765. The property was bought in 1847 by Philip Hine, the wine merchant.

The Walnuts, built c.1820 has lias ashlar walls. This, together with the house next door and also No. 6 Prout Bridge were at one time owned by the Daniel family, and a Dr John Daniel was living at a house on this site in 1775.

Minster View, in Shorts Lane, is built of stone with a red-brick façade. On the side wall is a plaque with the date 1781 and the name John Brown. The house later became the home of the Keech family, monumental masons.

The Old Vicarage was built 1859–61 in asymmetrical Victorian Gothic style. This is the Emminster Parsonage of Thomas Hardy's *Tess of the d'Urbervilles* to which Tess made her fruitless journey in search of Angel Clare.

Minster View, Shorts Lane, with its smart red brick façade, once favoured over the local stone of which the house is built.

Farrs, Whitcombe Road.

The Old Vicarage. This was Thomas Hardy's Emminster Parsonage.

The Parnham Estate

A mile from the town stands Parnham House. The Strode family was well established here following the arrival of Richard Strode in the fifteenth century. William Strode had done a certain amount of building by 1500, but the house was largely rebuilt by Robert Strode in the mid-seventeenth century. From this period date the hall, with its two porches, and the wing adjoining the hall on the north. A separate

Sir Henry Oglander, owner of Parnham House in the nineteenth century.

kitchen wing was built onto the northwest corner in the seventeenth century.

The Strode family were staunch Royalists during the Civil War. Before the war the inheritance had been disputed by Sir Richard Strode and his uncle, Sir John Strode. Sir John died before the beginning of the war but his wife, Lady Anne Strode, clung on to the estate with the help of the King's forces. In 1646 Fairfax and the New Model Army came to Parnham and although accounts of the incident vary Lady Anne was certainly killed by the sword in Parnham House itself.

In 1764 the estate passed to the Oglander family. When Sir William Oglander died in 1806 his son took the estate in hand and had many alterations made to the house under the direction of the renowned architect John Nash, who had built East Cowes Castle on the Isle of Wight and was a neighbour of the Oglanders. The Oglanders' ownership, which had lasted 130 years, ended with the death of Louisa, the widow of Sir William Oglander, in 1894.

In 1896 the estate was sold to Vincent Robinson. Hans Sauer owned the house in 1910 and the Great Hall was restored and many of the previous additions were swept away revealing the stone walls and oak ceiling timbers. The grounds were landscaped, terraces built and a lake dug. In 1913 it became the property of Mr and Mrs Edward Moorhouse. Their son, William Rhodes-Moorhouse VC, who died in the First World War and his son, also William, who was killed in the Battle of Britain, are buried in a private graveyard on a hillside above Parnham House.

Parnham House was bought by Hans Saur in the spring of 1910. He completely restored Parnham and the grounds were landscaped and a lake made by 'armies of men with wheelbarrows and spades.'

Workmen at Parnham. Charlie Gibbs is at the front on the right-hand side. c.1910.

Thought to be the demolition of the gates at Parnham in 1950. Left to right: Charlie Paul, Bert Gay, Percy Daw(e)?, Ray Poole.

The house had other owners and incarnations, including a country club in the late 1920s. It was requisitioned for military use during the Second World War, firstly as an army hospital and later as the headquarters of the 16th Infantry Division of the American Army. It was a residential home in the 1950s and in 1976 became the home and workshop of the celebrated furniture maker John Makepeace. Under the auspices of The Parnham Trust he founded The School for Craftsmen in Wood, which opened in 1977. At the time of writing the house is again in private ownership.

Wynford, No. 11 Whitcombe Road, dates from the late-eighteenth century. In about 1900 it was known as Whitcombe Cottage and was occupied by the minister of the Congregational church, Revd Pointer, who is seen here with his family.

Above: *The Yews dates from the late-eighteenth century. It was once occupied by the Revd James Woodward Scott, curate of Beaminster. Originally known as Niles Tenement, having been held by the Nile family, it became known as The Yews in the mid-1880s.*

Right: *A characterful building with some details predating the 1781 fire. A. & E. Toleman, who had these premises in the mid-nineteenth century, were bell hangers, locksmiths, painters, plumbers, tin plate workers, agricultural agents and sanitary engineers. It has been an antique shop and is now Pickwicks, a pub/restaurant.*

Ham's Plot, No. 6 Bridport Road, was once owned by Thomas Fox. The house dates from the seventeenth century and was considerably altered c.1830.

London House, Hogshill Street, has strong Victorian details. In 1880 Edwin Coombs had his draper's shop here which was taken over in 1895 by Arthur E. Reynolds. It was a café in the 1950s and is now an estate agents and a private dwelling.

Above: *Hamilton Lodge, built in the late-nineteenth century. John Hamilton, woollen manufacturer from about 1800–30, had a factory on this site.*

Right: *Knowle Cottage, Shorts Lane, dates from the nineteenth century. It is in two separate parts; a cottage fronting the road and a house behind.*

Edgeley Cottage, No. 9 Whitcombe Road, dates from the mid-seventeenth century. It was known as East Road Cottage in 1885 when James Read lived there.

A Portrait of Hooke and Hooke Court

Hooke is a small village about three miles east of Beaminster with a current population of about 130. The village is in the valley that runs from Toller Down to Maiden Newton, where the River Hooke joins the River Frome. It has 18 springs so fresh water is in abundant supply.

The village is about 400 metres from an Iron Age ridgeway joining Eggardon, a large Iron Age fort, to the ridgeway that served much of the South West. With the abundant supply of fresh water it is a strong possibility that these early inhabitants would have built wooden platforms above marshy ground from which to collect water. A large area containing Romano-British tiles from the period AD200–400 has been found in a south-facing field suggesting a Romano-British farm.

Hooke is mentioned in Domesday as having a mill. Its name derives from the 1086 name for the village, La Hoc. The Old English *hoc* means a projecting corner, or sharp bend in a stream; the name suits the topography well.

According to records there were originally two villages, the second being Stapleford. The parishes of Stapleford and Hooke were merged in 1361. Stapleford is one of Dorset's vanished villages and there are three different opinions regarding its exact location. One of the possible sites is at Knights-in-the-Bottom, the site of a settlement. It is the location of the village's earliest recorded inn, The Masons Arms, a drover's and a smuggler's inn.

From records and a recent excavation it would appear that Hooke Court was a very important building from the thirteenth to the sixteenth century. In 1344 the Cyfrewast family had it crenellated (pseudo-battlements put on the top of the building) and added a moat and a dovecote.

The patron saint of the church is St Giles. He is patron saint of blacksmiths, beggars, cripples, and a multitude of sicknesses and illnesses. The statue was carved in 1878 by Ben Grassby and won a silver medal at the Dorset Industrial Exhibition that year.

HOOKE CHURCH
SWAGGER ARCH

The swagger arch in St Giles Church. The estate passed through female members of the line at various times. One of these was Elizabeth Cheney who married Sir John Coleshill. The swagger arch either celebrates their marriage or their ownership of Hooke Court between 1510 and 1520.

Part of the moat still exists and the foundations of the old house and the dovecote were found during excavations in 2006. It is interesting to note that permission to crenellate and have a moat installed required permission from the King – and the owners needed to be rich. The buildings had a gatehouse with guest accommodation, each room having a separate toilet (not flushing!), another wing and a large hall in a third building. The building was further enhanced by the Staffords who followed in the late-fourteenth century.

By this time the mill was called a fulling mill and used for combing and pressing wool. The Staffords built the church in about 1410 after the merger of the two parishes. It had many fifteenth-century features and a particularly good sixteenth-century swagger arch and the usual gallery. By 1550 it also had a tower. The photograph from 1870 shows the remaining stump, though it is unclear whether the tower was pulled down or if it collapsed.

The church was modernised in the nineteenth century, the gallery removed and a small vestry added. In one niche is a statue of St Giles. The statue was carved in stone in 1878 by Ben Grassby and won a silver medal at the Dorset Industrial Exhibition; the medal was presented by the Earl of Shaftesbury. It is not certain how the statue came to Hooke.

The estate was home to a deer park from at least the early-fourteenth century. Queen Elizabeth I had a survey of such parks carried out and it was discovered that Hooke was one of only a dozen remaining active deer parks in Dorset. Its size would suggest that the deer were rounded up with dogs and netted for food. It became derelict when Hooke Court was burned down during the Civil War and sold to a Thomas Jarboys. Other than this short interlude, the estate stayed within the same family from 1281 to 1917. It would appear that the oak used for palings around the deer park was sold by Thomas Jarboys rather than used for repairs. When the restored King Charles II returned the estate to the Marquis of Winchester a new site was chosen for the deer park.

There are only a few pre-Victorian houses left in the village. During Victoria's reign it was mainly an agricultural village with a population of about 240 and was so poor that it received a specific mention in an article in *The Times* on Monday 3 August 1846:

There is also a parish called Hook, in the neighbourhood of Beaminster, to which my attention was directed since I left that town, and which I have since had an opportunity of visiting. The nature of distress which exists here will also justify a few remarks. The wages of the labourer here are the very lowest on which life can be supported, and the dwellings appropriated to him are, in most instances,

absolutely ruinous and demand the assistance of props inside and out to keep them from the ground. I have some reason to suppose my arrival in the village was in some degree expected and prepared for. In the first house at which I applied for information, I found a young woman of about 20 or 21 years of age, and a child about eight years, the rest of the family being absent on their daily occupation. She informed me that she was the eldest daughter of the inmate of the cottage. I inquired what was the amount of her father's earnings. She 'did not know'. I next asked what rent they paid for the house. To this she pleaded ignorance. I then ventured to ask how many children her father had. She 'could not recollect'. But the child who was present, to the last query answered in an undertone 'six', for which she was immediately reprimanded and silenced. In general I have found throughout my inquiries no unwillingness to afford information. The labourer generally seems happy to have an opportunity of relating his grievances, and in general, I think, the chief thing to be guarded against is exaggeration. In the case I have just mentioned I feel little doubt but that strict injunctions of silence had been laid on this man and his family. I, however, discovered others whom want had rendered more communicative, and who afforded me long and minute accounts of distress and poverty. It is impossible to conceive the miserable state in which the inhabitants of this village pass their lives. They are the victims of every evil attendant upon want and insufficient lodging. The almost total absence of furniture is a conspicuous feature in this place. It generally consists of a couple of rough benches and a foundered table, the latter usually set against a wall in order to supply the deficiency of a leg.

Hooke Court was the manorial house, and the manorial court was held there until the establishment of the local authorities in the nineteenth century. By the mid-nineteenth century Hooke Court had become a farmhouse and in the later nineteenth century the Earl of Sandwich decided that it would make a good shooting box, where his friends could come as a shooting party for a couple of weeks. In order to impress these visitors there were bridges put across the fords, the houses were rebuilt, and a new house for the rector, a new farmhouse for the farmer who had been at Hooke Court were also constructed. Among the visitors was the Prince of Wales and, local tradition has it, the Prince's mistress Lillie Langtry. A shooting accident was recorded in the *Bridport News* in 1886 when Col Papillon was shot in the eye. Fortunately, as the paper revealed, there was '... no cause for fearing any serious consequence.'!

From 1900 to 1902 Hooke Court was a convalescent home for injured and sick officers from the Boer War. Over 50 officers stayed there looked after by the Earl and a masseur.

Above: *After the Boer War there were parties held at Hooke Court usually involving a game of croquet. The Earl of Sandwich is seen here.*

Left: *The Prince of Wales was one of the visitors to Hooke Court for shooting parties. He is seen here with the Earl of Sandwich outside Hooke Court in about 1900. Tradition in the village suggests that his mistress, Lillie Langtry, accompanied him on these visits and stayed at a house in the village.*

Shooting party at Hooke Court in November 1888. Left to right, back row: Col A. Paget, Lieut R.W. Gordon Gilmour, Col A. Egerton; front row: Hon St J. Aubyn, Earl of Sandwich, Captain Hon V. Montagu.

Left: *Major Mullins VC, a South African officer who convalesced at Hooke Court during the Boer War.*

Right: *The forge was moved to the new cottages near the church in about 1900. Mr Paull, seen here, was the blacksmith. The telephone kiosk (left) was brought to the village on a horse-drawn cart to be placed in the position shown in 1937.*

Skittles, c.1937, in Glebe field where the houses in Paulet Close now stand.

The village had up to three mills in the nineteenth century; one produced thread and hemp employing about 60 people until it was burned down. The last mill was on the original site of the Domesday mill and at the time of writing is a private house. The owner at the beginning of the twentieth century had a large watercress farm that has more recently become a trout-breeding farm.

There was a school from 1858 that was eventually closed in 1947. There were a blacksmith, a Post Office and shop run before the Second World War by the blacksmith and his wife. The village inn

closed in 1960 along with the Post Office and shop.

In the middle of the twentieth century Hooke Court was owned by the Anglican Franciscan monks as a boarding-school for boys with behavioural and emotional problems. In 2007 it is a private nursery school and a preparatory school, and also provides residential accommodation for school field trips and adult accommodation for families.

The village is now the home of many young professional and business people with several working from home. There are only two farmers and three smallholders.

Above: *Hooke Church of England School, 1937.*

Below: *Oblique aerial photograph of Hooke Court taken in about 1950. The remnants of the moat can be seen. There is a suggestion that the building to the right, demolished in the late 1950s, was the gatehouse.*

Above: *Man with his dog and two Dorset Horn sheep. All the images on this page probably come from the 1920s/'30s.*

Right: *A shepherd bringing sheep and lambs out of the fold at Stoke Abbott.*

Below: *Sheep shearing.*

Chapter 5

'Fold, Fallow and Plough'

Agriculture has always been of great importance in Dorset, and until comparatively recently most of the people living in the county were directly or indirectly involved in farming or one of its associated trades.

When did it begin? There is evidence of early farming in the county from around 3500BC when the Neolithic settlers, who kept animals and grew crops of wheat and barley, began clearance of the natural forest. Few of their precise sites are now known, but there have been at least two finds of Neolithic axeheads in the vicinity of Beaminster so their presence here is fairly certain. By the Bronze Age (c.2000BC) the countryside was already being heavily utilised. The population continued to rise during the Iron Age which followed, and both high- and low-lying land was inhabited and farmed. Dorset was the centre of the tribe of the Durotriges who achieved a reasonably sophisticated way of life with a developed agricultural and pastoral farming economy.

The Romans arrived into an already well occupied and cultivated landscape. With their imposition of peace on the warring Celtic tribes, the local population continued to rise and yet more land was brought into cultivation, some on the higher chalklands. However, towards the end of the Roman period there seems to have been a withdrawal from these uplands. This may have been due to technical advances in agriculture, which enabled new tracts of land in the valleys and lowlands to be settled and cultivated more intensively.

The Saxon invasion came late to our part of Dorset and it has been suggested that after their initial defeat the Romano-British population lived on in peace and comparative prosperity with their conquerors. Many land units or estates that date back to Roman times or earlier continued as before. From the evidence of the 30 or more Saxon charters in existence for Dorset it is clear that many of the boundaries of early parishes were already in place before the Norman Conquest, as were the boundaries of estates.

The Saxons had always been associated with the open-field system, with its pattern of long, narrow, unfenced strips, divided between two or more large fields and worked in common. It used to be assumed that the Saxons brought this system with them but it is now thought that it developed gradually over the centuries after their arrival. In West Dorset there are many places where there is no evidence that common fields existed, the type of landscape here indicating small farmsteads carved out of the forest or waste-land and directly enclosed. This is particularly so in areas such as Marshwood Vale.

At the time of the enclosure of 1809 there were two large common fields adjoining Beaminster West Down, comprising 290 acres. The original common fields of Beaminster would certainly have been very much larger. Marie Eedle in *A History of Beaminster* suggests that in the early Middle Ages, due to pressure of population and subsistence farming, there was probably more land under the plough in West Dorset than there has been at any other time. There are several areas of lynchets on the slopes of White Sheet Hill, pointing to an extension of cultivation down the hillside in a time of land shortage. It is impossible to date these exactly but they could be as early as the eleventh century.

During the later medieval period in Dorset there was a general contraction of arable land and a great increase in sheep farming. The local Dorset Horn sheep were characterised by their ability to breed nearly all the year round. Sheep were valued not only for the meat and wool they produced but for their contribution to the fertility of the land; not for nothing have they been called 'walking dung-carts'. The vast flocks in Dorset were commented on by all travellers in the county, but while sheep dominated the higher chalklands, the other main agricultural occupations in West Dorset were cattle rearing and dairy farming, the milk produced being turned into butter or cheese. On the whole the sixteenth and seventeenth centuries were prosperous times for farmers in this area, as is made clear from the probate inventories of the period. The numbers of fine stone farmhouses dating from this time are still to be seen and tell their own story.

The market in Beaminster was still functioning in the early-seventeenth century, and presumably trade was increasing as a new Market House was built. However, after the fire of 1684 it never regained its former importance. By this time the larger markets tended to specialise – Chard in cattle, Crewkerne in cattle and sheep, Bridport in linen, hemp, rope and twine. Hemp and linen also figured large at the market in Yeovil, as did butter and cheese. Yeovil was an important market for this area of Dorset.

The Growth of Local Crops and Dairy

The importance of crops of flax and hemp must not be underestimated. Both crops were grown all over Dorset in medieval times and there was a flourishing

Hand-milking at Hill Farm, South Perrott.

rope and net industry in Bridport. Sail-cloth manu-facture was also important, using the locally grown flax, and this centred around Beaminster, Broadwindsor and Bridport. Acts of Parliament to promote the growing of the two crops were passed

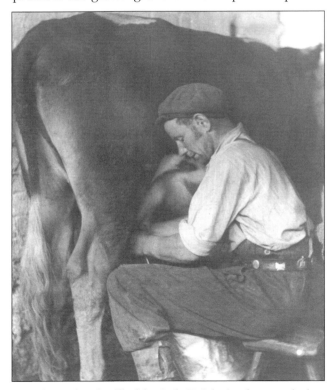

Cow being hand-milked by Jack Knight in the cow-shed at Broadenham Farm, Salway Ash, 1946.

by the Tudors and the industry grew apace. The growing of flax and hemp fitted in well with dairy farming, and the soil, particularly between Bridport and Beaminster, was very suitable for their cultiva-tion. In 1794 Netherbury was the leading parish in flax production and in 1812 Beaminster was included in a list of hemp-growing parishes. The Napoleonic Wars saw peak production of these products, but later these crops declined due to foreign competition.

Potatoes, which were also grown as an arable crop on richer soils must have taken the place of hemp and flax in some places where their cultivation was discontinued. It is interesting to note that potatoes were only introduced in gardens from about 1770, but soon became grown widely as a field crop, and indeed, in the nineteenth century, became a vital part of farm labourers' diets.

Most of the land in West Dorset was grassland in the eighteenth century and though some sheep were kept on the higher ground the main emphasis was on dairying. A widespread practice in Dorset was the renting of dairies. Under this system the farmer provided the cows together with the necessary pasture and winter fodder, as well as a house for the dairyman and a dairy, in return for an annual rent per cow, while the dairyman made his profit from the sale of milk, butter and cheese. (A description of such a rented dairy is given by Thomas Hardy in *Tess of the d'Urbervilles*.) The system was condemned by the agricultural 'improver' but continued to be common in the region until well into the nineteenth century.

Eighteenth-Century Technology and Developments in Farming

Improvements in agriculture, which had begun in the eighteenth century, began to gather pace. New and improved strains of wheat, barley, oats and rye, together with new methods of cultivation and crop rotation, improved yields. Iron equipment was used in place of the traditional wooden ploughs and harrows, as well as the new drills and threshing and winnowing machines. At Langdon Farm in Beaminster, Richard Bridge had a two-horse threshing machine in the early 1800s.

Land drainage was also greatly improved, helped by the availability of cheap clay drainage pipes. Tremendous strides too had been made with attention to selective breeding and improvements in livestock with the introduction of new breeds of sheep, pigs and cattle. There were also new developments in butter and cheese making, and the coming of the railways meant the opening up of new markets for these products. Later in the century greatly improved machinery was beginning to be available, and by 1872 ploughing and threshing using steam power was becoming more common on the large arable farms.

Dorset Horn Sheep, c.1940-50.

Farmer and bull. The pole is connected with a chain to the ring in the bull's nose, c.1930.

The formation of agricultural clubs and societies to spread information and encourage higher standards indicates the amount of enthusiasm for agricultural improvement. Pre-eminent in this area was the Bath and West of England Society whose influence on the whole region was profound. Very influential in the Beaminster area was the Melplash Agricultural Society which was formed in 1847, one of the oldest in the country. It still continues and holds a one-day agricultural show every August, now held on a site at West Bay.

A Struggling Industry

This era of optimism and prosperity, which, incidentally, did not extend to the farm labourer who existed throughout the period on an incredibly low wage, came to an end during the 1870s. The previous chapter on Hooke gives an account of the plight of the farm labourers in Dorset. Several factors contributed to the severe depression in farming which lasted until 1914 and was marked by very great hardship and distress among farmers. The causes included a succession of wet, cold springs and summers, followed by disastrously poor harvests. The poor grain yields coincided with a drop in corn prices following an influx of cheap corn from America and Canada. The appalling weather also hit livestock farmers, with foot-rot ravishing sheep flocks and a general shortage of good quality hay for winter feed.

In the face of competition from imported cheese and butter many dairy farmers abandoned their production altogether and concentrated on the supply of liquid milk, either to London or other large towns if there was a convenient railway link, or to the newly formed cheese factories. However, in the Beaminster rural district in 1908 there were still 70 dairy farms converting their milk to butter and cheese. In 1904 the West Surrey Central Dairy Company established a milk factory in Beaminster, producing dried milk products marketed as 'Cow and Gate Pure English Milk Powder'.

There was a great decline in the acreage of arable land due to the agricultural depression and a corresponding increase in the acreage of permanent pasture. This in turn meant the demand for farm labour was greatly reduced and between 1871 and 1911 the number of labourers in Dorset fell by 31 per cent. It is therefore no surprise that the population in villages hereabouts endured a sharp decline. The early-twentieth century had already witnessed a vast increase in the machinery deployed on farms, and this too had led to a decreased demand for labour.

Farming During and Between the Wars

By the outbreak of the First World War the increasing use of steam power, stationary oil engines, modern fencing – especially barbed wire – new artificial

Threshing in full swing. The man pictured here is bagging the corn. This picture and the one below come from Broadenham Farm, Salway Ash, 1949.

Threshing gang and family with the threshing machine.

Reaper on the left. The corn has been cut and a good bag of rabbits shot in the harvest field. Tom Willment from Pineapple Dairy, Salway Ash, is second from the left. c.1940-50.

manures and foodstuffs, and a greatly increased range of mass-produced implements was altering the pace and character of farming. During the war tractors (largely American makes) appeared on some larger farms. After the war British-made tractors began to appear on more farms and gradually replaced horses. It was a slow process and even when tractors became cheaper and more easily available in the 1930s many farmers preferred to stay with their horses.

The introduction of the Hosier Milking Bail system brought a big change to dairy farms. This consisted of an easily transportable milking-parlour or bail which could be used in the fields. It meant that lands at some distance from the farm could be used for dairy herds providing there was a piped water supply. This new freedom made a great difference and these prefabricated bails became popular all over the West Country.

With the First World War came a temporary period of prosperity to Dorset farms, but by the mid-1920s imports had all resumed and many Dorset farmers were only saved from ruin by the market for liquid milk. They were also considerably helped by the setting up of the Milk Marketing Board in 1933. There was not much incentive to invest in new equipment or machinery, but by 1941 there were 259 milking machines in the county. These, however, were mainly on large farms, and neither tractors nor milking machines made much progress in Dorset until after the outbreak of the Second World War.

The Second World War revolutionised farming in the county. The priority by this time was to grow as much home-produced foodstuffs as possible and various government directives and incentives were introduced to encourage farmers to increase production as an essential part of the war effort. The labour situation on farms was considerably changed, first by the arrival of the Land Girls of the Women's Land Army to take the place of men who had been called up, and later by the employment of German and Italian prisoners of war. Replacement of horses by tractors increased rapidly and many new implements designed for use with tractors were introduced.

Thousands of acres were ploughed up for corn and potato production. Flax-growing was again encouraged in West Dorset and by 1941 some 500 acres of flax was being grown to supply the Fontmell Industries Mill at Netherbury.

The demand for home-grown food during the war meant that the period from 1939 to 1949 saw wide-ranging changes continuing to accelerate. In particular, mechanisation had almost entirely replaced horses, while combine harvesters and milking machines with the use of electricity had become almost universal. Farm sizes continued to increase, especially on the chalklands.

A Century of Farming

J.H. Bettey, in his 1996 book *Man and the Land:Farming in Dorset*, states that in Dorset the Agricultural Revolution occurred in the last 150 years:

A farmer from any part of Dorset in 1850 would find today that almost every aspect of farming life had been transformed, and that the old characteristic features of farming in the county have disappeared. The old constants of soils and weather, seed-time and harvest of course remain, but all else has changed. On the chalklands the great flocks of folding sheep have vanished, the vast expanses of downland have been enclosed by hedges and converted into arable, the water-meadows are disused and undreamt of yields of wheat are obtained... ever more complex machines enable these huge crops to be produced with far less manual toil and by a tiny proportion of the labour force which was once employed. Very few people work on the land, but a very large proportion of the population is interested and concerned at what happens to it. Conservation and ecology are important, and organic farming is increasing.

One cannot help but wonder – what of the future? Where will farmers diversify next after alpaca and buffalo, bio-fuel and medicinal herbs, lavender and vineyards?

Above: *Rick thatching at Broadenham Farm, Salway Ash in 1949.*

Left: *Rick thatching at Broadenham Farm, Salway Ash in 1949.*

Building the base of a rick with an elevator. Broadenham Farm, Salway Ash, 1949.

Elevator at Melplash, c.1920. The horse walked in a circle driving the mechanism, which transferred the power to the elevator enabling the stack to be built. The man holding the horse on the right is Mr A. Hawkins.

Axnoller farmhouse, 1891. Mr A. Gillingham is in the helmet, with Gladys on the left.

The cottages at Axnoller, c.1899, with mare and foal. The man in the pith helmet is A. Gillingham.

Above: *Massey Ferguson 165 in 1967. The tyres were filled with water and weights placed in front and behind the tractor to enable it to remain stable on the steep slope. The driver is Ernie Norris of Melplash who worked on the same farm for over 40 years.*

Right: *A countryman, c.1900.*

Below: *The Rockley Herd of Guernseys at Melplash Court Farm, 1956.*

Below right: *Feeding the hens, at Broadenham Farm, Salway Ash, 1948/9.*

Haymaking, c.1910.

Charles Reuben Lush outside Mapperton House. He was probably employed there in 1908. Later he became whipper-in to the Cattistock Hunt.

The front porch showing the Brodrepp arms.

View from the porch of Mapperton House with the eagle gate piers.

The overmantel in the library of Mapperton House, showing the arms of James I.

The overmantel in the hall with the arms of Paulet.

Mapperton Gardens, showing the glasshouses, c.1910. Mapperton House can be seen in the background.

Mapperton: The Hidden Valley

The name Mapperton means 'maple tree farm' and its first recorded mention is in the Domesday Survey of 1086 when it was listed as two parcels of land. One of these, North Mapperton, was in the parish of Beaminster and was held by Arnulf. The other, South Mapperton, was held by William of Mohun and consisted of the later manors of Mapperton and Coltleigh. We know, therefore, that there were already thriving Saxon settlements here in the eleventh century, but the finding of a Bronze Age axehead at Marsh Farm indicates that this favoured valley was settled by people of a much earlier period.

The site of the original village is unknown, but the Dorset historian, Hutchins, states that the tenants of the two manors of Mapperton and Coltleigh 'almost dying of the plague in 1666, the tenements fell into the lord's hand, and all have been pulled down.' The victims are said to have been buried on a hill in sight of Netherbury, the mother church. Mapperton people were normally buried at Netherbury because in its own church-yard the rock is so near the surface that the digging of graves is virtually impossible.

The Manor House

Mapperton House, one of the loveliest manor houses in Dorset, was built by Robert Morgan between 1540 and 1550 to replace an earlier house

Mapperton Gardens. The neo-classical Orangery was added between 1966 and 1968 by Victor Montagu.

The Cattistock Hunt gather outside Mapperton House, c.1910.

71

on the site, probably built by the Bretts who were already established at Mapperton by the twelfth century. Until 1919 Mapperton House never passed for sale. For nearly eight-and-a-half centuries it was in the hands of four families: the Bretts, Morgans, Brodrepps and Comptons, passing through the female line.

In 1425 Robert Morgan of Mapperton was granted a 'bonnet patent' by Henry VI, allowing him to wear his bonnet at all times, even in the King's presence:

... forasmoche as wee bee credibly informed that owr well beloved Robert Morgan, esquire for diverse infirmities which he hath in his hedde cannot conveniently without grete daungier be discovered of the same.

A similar licence was issued to a later Robert Morgan in 1522 by Henry VIII.

If these Roberts suffered from cold heads, in contrast, the Johns of the family seem to have been hotheaded! In 1533 John Morgan killed a man called Anchret Palmer, but received a pardon as he successfully pleaded that he had acted in self-defence. In 1580 his grandson, John also killed a man, his brother-in-law Nicholas Turberville, and he was hanged in consequence.

Of Robert Morgan's manor house, built between 1540 and 1550, only the northern range remains more or less unaltered, except for the garden front. Within it there are two bedrooms with fine Tudor ceilings, one of which is the Hampton Court type with pendants. There is also an original Tudor ceiling in the drawing-room which shows the lions of the Bretts and the *fleur-de-lys* of the Morgans. There was formerly an inscription in the hall, probably over the fireplace, which read, 'Robert Morgan and Mary built this house in their own lifetime at their own charge and cost.' They then added a contemporary moralising ditty:

What they spent, that they lent,
What they gave, that they have,
What they left, that they lost.

The hall range was probably rebuilt in about 1670 and given a new front by the second Richard Brodrepp, who also added the stable range and gate piers. Above the outside of the porch are the Brodrepp arms. Inside the porch by the shell-head niches are found the initials R.B. with the date 1666. The fourth Richard Brodrepp altered the north wing in the mid-eighteenth century, giving it a classical façade and inserting a Georgian staircase. The overmantel in the hall dated 1604 with the Paulet coat of arms came from Melplash Court, as did the overmantel in the

library with the arms of James I.

The gardens to the east are tucked into a steep north/south combe and descend from the very formal gardens to an arboretum. At the northern end is Fountain Court, an Italianate garden of stone, grass, topiary and water. South of this are two rectangular pools flanked by tall clipped yew trees. The gradual transition from formal garden to landscape was the work of two twentieth-century owners of Mapperton, both great gardeners, Mrs Labouchere who bought the house in 1919 and Victor Montagu who purchased it in 1955.

All Saints' Church and Rectory

This church dates from the twelfth century, though the nave was rebuilt in 1704 and extensive repairs were carried out in 1846 when the windows were restored, the gallery removed and the porch added. The southwest tower, now below roof level, and the blocked west doorway originate from the fifteenth century. The church's special features are the warm golden Ham stone of which it is built and the sixteenth- and seventeenth-century roundels of glass inserted in the plain glass of the nave windows. There is an imposing monument to Richard Brodrepp and his children by Peter Scheemakers, who also created Shakespeare's monument in Westminster Abbey.

Mapperton rectory was built between 1699 and 1703 and there is a full set of building accounts for it. Work began with the opening of a rubble stone quarry in the parsonage orchard. Two men were continuously employed for five months there and the stone – Inferior Oolite – was then left to weather for 18 months.

Building proper began in 1701 and the house was finished in 1703 and occupied by the September of that year. It was built for the Revd John Powell who became vicar of South Mapperton in 1698. His name is inscribed over the front door and on the stables. The total cost was £246.16s.4d., of which £20 was for the stone from Ham Hill that was used for the door and window surrounds (the more local stone was not suitable for the finer work). Half the expense of this stone lay in the cost of carriage from Ham Hill.

A Catholic Martyr

Coltleigh is a farm in Mapperton and in the sixteenth century had a famous resident. John Munden was born here in 1543 to a family known for its Roman Catholic sympathies. At this time life was becoming more difficult for Catholics and penal laws were enacted against them. There were, nevertheless, many Catholics and sympathisers to be found. Some of them kept their heads well down, others such as John Munden became high profile Catholics who faced heavy fines, loss of property and imprisonment.

On leaving Oxford, John became a schoolmaster and was appointed to the school at Netherbury in 1565. In 1580 he went abroad to study divinity and was ordained in Rome in 1582. He returned to England on the Jesuit Mission, a dangerous undertaking as the presence of a priest in this country was treated as an act of high treason. He was arrested in 1583, spent some months in the Tower, and condemned to death with four others. They were dragged to Tyburn on hurdles and hanged,

drawn and quartered. John Munden was the last to die and was forced to watch the execution of his fellow priests before he suffered the same barbarous fate.

The Posy Tree

This is the tree on the right-hand side of the lane between Mapperton and Netherbury about which there are various legends. Of these, the story most likely to be true is one that tells of some 80 people of Mapperton dying of plague in 1582. Their bodies were taken to Netherbury for burial as was usual, as the ground at Mapperton churchyard was unsuitable and Netherbury was the mother church.

On this occasion, however, the inhabitants of Netherbury, not wishing to have the bodies of plague victims buried in their village, gathered at the tree armed with staves and refused to let the Mapperton villagers pass. The bodies were therefore taken to a site on Warren Hill nearby and buried in a mass grave there. Over it was planted a copse of conifers so that the land would not be disturbed. It was said that survivors gathered wild flowers and herbs to ward off the plague as the bodies were taken up the lane to the burial place; possibly their posies were laid by the tree or hung on it.

An interesting item from *Dorset Upalong Downalong* on this subject reads as follows:

Box hedges were planted as a preventative of the plague. Box yew and rosemary were supposed to be useful for this purpose, and when the plague came to Netherbury in the sixteenth century, box hedges were planted everywhere.

Mythe

Mythe is a hamlet half a mile downstream from Mapperton. Its name means 'the confluence of two streams', and there was once a mill here by the ford. Nothing now is left of the row of deserted cottages mentioned in *A Mythe Childhood* written

The etched window dedicated to John Munden, a Roman Catholic martyr from Coltleigh.

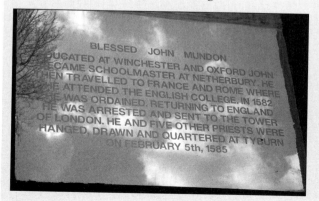

Detail from the etched window in the Roman Catholic church at Shortmoor, Beaminster.

Cottages at Mythe.

by Florence Stephens. She lived at Mythe for three years from 1929, during the agricultural depression. Her father was aged 67 and they lived on his son's wages of 25s. a week on top of his pension of 10s. She recalled, 'There was just enough for the shopping, but hardly anything left over for Mum.' There was a certain freedom, it wasn't all idyllic:

You didn't have to worry about traffic. We used to wash our hair in the spring below the sheep dip, where there was a wooden plank, and swing across the stream from a rope in the beech tree.

Reminiscences of Farming

The following description of life on Marsh Farm, Mapperton was written by Dick Berry, who came here in 1941 to learn farming with Mr and Mrs Ralph Cox:

Milking then [1941] was done by hand, sixty cows, some old red Devons with great wide horns with brass knobs on them. The rest were crossed with a Shorthorn bull except for one old cow, the only Friesian and the best milker of them all. We tied them up in the cowstalls and hand fed and watered them during the winter months.

Implements were limited and he describes how 'old Frank' used only a two-furrow plough with three horses, a cultivator, some drags and harrows, a roller and a drill. Grass seed and fertiliser were sown by hand or with a fiddle.

An early Bronze Age flat axe from Mapperton.

When high ricks were constructed 'Kitty the cob' walked round and round 'when she thought fit' to power the large elevator.

The sheep really took pride of place at Mapperton. There was a large flock of Dorset Downs lambing in February to March, the lambs selling mainly at the September sales in Dorchester. At Poundbury Fair the price of a six month old lamb would be less than we pay now for a few chops. As a young man, Ralph would drive the flock of lambs to Dorchester from Beaminster, taking two or three days, but there were lorries to do that job in 1941.

Mapperton rectory, built 1699–1703.

Chapter 6

Readin', Ritin' an' Reckonin'

The earliest references to a school in Beaminster are of a schoolmaster called Lancelot Crabb in 1634 and items bought for a schoolhouse which appear in the churchwardens' accounts for 1651 and 1663.

In 1682 a prosperous spinster, Frances Tucker, left in her will £20 a year (taken from the income of her farm, South Mapperton), for the maintenance of a schoolmaster to teach 20 of the poorest boys of the parish of Beaminster. He was to 'take care of their manners', 'catechise them, teach them to read and write' and 'in some competent measure to cast an account'. She also made provision in her will for the trustees to fire the schoolmaster if he 'shall be negligent loud or debauched' and appoint a new one.

A further £30 a year was to be used to fund apprenticeships for three or four of these boys, including one or two to be sent to sea. Due to wrangles over the bequest the first schoolmaster, William Coombe, was only appointed in 1703. Joseph Harbin took over as schoolmaster in 1709 followed by John Harbin in 1711 and from 1715 the Revd Samuel Hood (later to become the father of the two distinguished Admirals

This portrait, c.1660, of Frances Tucker who founded a school in Beaminster in the seventeenth century still hangs in the school today.

Hood). The school was in an upper room of an 'annex' attached to the southwest corner of the church, which was the location of an apparently supernatural event.

A Ghostly Tale

John Guppy was the schoolmaster when something strange was experienced by several pupils. The story revolves around John Daniel, a sickly pupil born in 1714, whose mother had died soon after he was born and whose father remarried shortly afterwards. His father then died and John inherited 5s. and a part-tenancy of lands consisting of five acres of pasture and one acre of arable land. He was not to benefit from this inhertance for very long because in May 1728, having been sent out one day to see to his step-mother's cows he failed to return home. He was found dead the following morning on a small islet in the nearby river. His odd posture and marks on his neck and body suggested foul play but nevertheless he was buried in the churchyard without an inquest.

On a Saturday morning about three weeks later John Guppy dismissed the class. Three or four boys stayed to clean and sweep the school as usual. Then they heard a noise like a small bell being struck in the church, which sounded as though it were coming nearer and nearer. They ran out of the gallery and down the stairs to tell their friends who were playing in the churchyard that they thought someone was in the schoolroom. One of the boys climbed up and, through the door, he saw the apparition of a white coffin with brass nails and a piece of tape hanging from a coffin handle laid on one of the writing desks. He fell back but more pupils went up to look and saw John Daniel sitting and writing in his usual place in his normal school clothes. One of the boys who recognised him was his younger brother Isaac who shouted, 'There sits our John... I'll throw a stone at him.' The boys tried to dissuade him but he threw it and at once the church became very dark even though it was light outside. The apparition disappeared and the boys ran away in terror.

When they told their tale, suspicions were raised that the boy had been murdered. An inquest was organised and John Daniel's body was exhumed. The jury heard the evidence and their verdict was that the boy had been strangled. Nobody was ever charged. This might have been the end of the story but for the appearance of a second apparition about six weeks after the first. This time, during a church

Beaminster Community Play, 1987.

service, a reputable young girl saw a woman push open the door leading to the stairs to the schoolroom. She told her master who went towards the door which slammed shut as though pulled violently. There was no draught and no sign of anyone there who could have shut it. The girl's description of the woman everybody agreed was exactly that of John Daniel's dead mother, Hannah, but the girl had not even been born when Hannah died so could never have seen her!

This tale was dramatised in *Crackling Angels*, Beaminster's community play first performed in the parish church in March 1987.

A strange postscript to this tale occurred during the restorations in the church in 2006. A workman heard a bang on the south door and saw a person's shadow through a crack under the door. He looked outside but nobody was there. Then a dark figure, whose presence could not be logically explained, was seen in the church and the following morning the trail of a child's footprints were discovered in sand that had been laid for paving and the word PEACE written in the sand, yet nothing had been noticed the previous evening. Two days later the workmen heard and felt a howling gale coming under the west door but when they looked outside it was flat calm. A hoax – or another ghost?

The History of Schooling in Beaminster

In the early 1730s the school transferred to a thatched building on the south side of the churchyard which burnt down in 1781. Betty, daughter of the school-master William Pavy (or Paviott?), died in the fire. The school was rebuilt, this time with a tiled roof.

In 1784 the trustees decided that boys were only to be admitted between eight and ten years of age and could not stay at the school for longer than four years. By 1814 the building was considered too dilapidated and unsuitable for use as a school and it was demolished. To replace it a dwelling-house, a malt-house and half an acre of land at Shortmoor

were purchased and converted to a master's house and a schoolroom capable of accommodating 110 boys with a playground and an orchard. It was described as 'an ivy covered building with small windows of leaded lights, stone floor, white-washed walls and tiled roof.' The income for Tucker's Charity had increased and the roll was no longer restricted to the original 20 boys.

In the early years of the nineteenth century the only education available to poorer people in the town were the Tucker Free School for boys, a 'School of Industry', which ran for a short time at the work-house, and a Sunday School at the church. For the professional class some small private schools existed usually in a private house and often for only a handful of pupils. The sons and daughters of the gentry were taught at home by a tutor or governess, the boys eventually being sent away to school.

By the mid-nineteenth century Beaminster was a more populous place than 50 years before. There was a greater need for educational provision for the children of the better off and the number of private schools increased. J. Adam's school in St Mary Well Street and William May's in Fleet Street existed in 1824 as did a grammar school run by G.A. Henessey & Son which was taken over by William Gardner in 1832. At the latter boarders and day boys followed a curriculum of English language, reading, writing, arithmetic, composition and geography. Greek, Latin, merchants' accounts, drawing and land surveying were offered as additional optional subjects. Gardner's Academy, run in a private house, now called Shadrack House, in Shadrack Street, had closed by about 1868. There were also private girls' schools. Mrs John Warr's was in Hogshill Street and Elizabeth Nicholls ran a ladies' boarding-school in 1842 at Barton End in Fleet Street.

In 1830 a voluntary school for girls was established and affiliated to the National Society for Educating the Poor in the Principles of the Established Church. In 1835 the charge to each of the 50-plus girls was a penny a week – or twopence if taught writing. The school was in a room adjoining the workhouse in East Street. In 1860 boys joined the infant class there.

November 1865 saw the vicar of Beaminster, Revd Alfred Codd, requesting subscribers for a new school to be built for the girls and infants in Hogshill Street. Grants and local subscriptions were forth-coming and the building, comprising a schoolroom and smaller classroom for girls and a schoolroom for infant boys and girls, was opened on 3 September 1868. There was still an attendance charge for pupils. In 1872 the children of labourers paid 2d. a week, two children from the same family paying 3d. Later, higher fees were required from farmers and tradespeople. The school was then called the Girls' Elementary School.

A new boys' school was built, opening in 1875, on the old workhouse site in East Street. The new Boys'

Beaminster Girls Elementary School, c.1900.

The Infants' classroom at the Beaminster Girls Elementary School in Hogshill Street, c.1920.

Infants fancy dress at the Beaminster Girls Elementary School in 1940.

Beaminster Boys' Elementary School, East Street, c.1890. Thomas Crabbe is third from the right and Ernest Crabbe is second from the right, both in the back row.

Left: *Infants in Beaminster Girls Elementary School in 1936. The school cat clearly knows his place is by the stove.*

Below: *The Boys' Elementary School, East Street.*

Elementary School had one schoolroom and a class-room. The old Tucker Free School at Shortmoor was eventually demolished in 1883.

In 1871 a 'middle school' which would teach boys up to age 15 was proposed. It would teach reading and spelling, mensuration (measuring and calculating length area and volume) and land surveying, English grammar, composition and literature, history and geography, drawing, vocal music, Latin and/or French, and at least one branch of natural science. The new school in Beaminster and the older Netherbury Grammar School joined to become Beaminster & Netherbury Grammar School, first at Shortmoor and from 1882 at Barton End in Fleet Street. It closed in 1893 for a short time due to low pupil numbers, reopening under headmaster Mr Thomas Brown in January 1897 with 22 pupils at new premises built on the site of the old potteries in Hogshill Street. Tuition fees were £5 for boys under 13 and £6 for older boys with a charge of 5s. a term for stationery and games equipment; boarders were charged considerably more. Later that year a

'chemical laboratory' and workshop were erected to commemorate Queen Victoria's diamond jubilee. In 1904 girls were admitted as both boarders and day pupils and the girls from Miss Warr's private Brook House Ladies School transferred there in 1905.

A significant feature of Beaminster & Netherbury Grammar School was its agricultural curriculum taught by a specialist teacher from 1904. Four agricultural boarding scholarships were offered for the sons of Dorset farmers and there was great competition for these places. There was an Agricultural Field off Clay Lane up until 1933, which was divided into a number of plots on which experiments were undertaken trialling different fertilisers and varieties of vegetables. From 1919 to 1959 Mr A.W. Graveson taught botany and agriculture as subjects at the school. The school was enlarged in 1912 and there were 80 pupils by 1915.

In 1935 Tucker House, opposite the school on Hogshill Street, was opened as boarding accommodation for girls, who were housed there until 1953 when they moved to Woodlands on Bridport Road.

These children are in typical dress of the period 1900–1910. We have no information about the children or adults.

The old Grammar School at Netherbury.

The Grammar School curriculum included Agriculture, c.1950.

From 1939 war made its mark on school life as these extracts from the 1939 Christmas edition of the *Beaminster & Netherbury School Magazine* reveal:

> *... masters, parents and boys who worked, sometimes three and four hours a day during the holidays, digging ARP trenches for the School... Work has been continuing during the term by all the bigger boys and some of the smaller ones have managed to lend a hand when the eye of authority has been turned away...*
>
> *We have blacked out windows, we have dug more ground ready for vegetables, we have knitted and, apparently knitted and then done a little knitting.*

The Boys' Elementary School was also preparing for war, 'We dug two trenches at the Boys' School, either side of the school gardens', one pupil reminisced.

Teaching Today

Education reform continued and Beaminster & Netherbury Grammar School closed at Christmas 1962. The grammar school pupils, together with the boys and girls from the town and village elementary schools, formed the new Beaminster secondary school which opened in January 1963 under headmaster John Walton in new buildings at Newtown. It was renamed Beaminster Comprehensive School and later became a Technology College in 2001.

In a further twist to the story the Grammar School bell tower was relocated by builders C.G. Fry & Son Ltd to a new development at Poundbury, Dorchester.

In 1973 St Mary's Primary School was built in Clay Lane and the infants transferred there from the old girls' and infants' school in Hogshill Street.

Top left: *Rear aspect of the Beaminster and Netherbury Grammar School, c.1910–30.*

Top right: *The Grammar School, c.1910–30.*

Above: *The Grammar School, 1904. Left to right, back row: E. Frampton, ? Woodland, P. Hann, E.F. Bugler, ? Dommett, ? Edwards, H. Rogers, ? Moores; middle row: ? Popham, Revd A.A. Leonard MA, ? Brooks, C.W. Hall MA, ? Dicker, ? Swatridge; front row, seated on floor: C. Hann, ? Hicks, ? Dicker.*

Left: *Edward Tong, age 17. An agricultural scholar and boarder, he was head boy at the Grammar School. 1934 .*

Above: *The girls of the Grammar School, July 1919. This was taken by V. Allen, a Beaminster photographer.*

Right: *Stanley Gibbs in his Grammar School uniform on horseback in 1910. Some pupils rode to school, stabling their horses in the town during the school day.*

Below: *Form V Beaminster and Netherbury Grammar School, 1945. Left to right, back row: Keefe, Perry, Warren, ?, Taylor, Gill, Sims, Bryant; middle row: Pardey, M. Henderich?, Cuffe, L. Pitcher, Hill, Shepherd; front row: Rita Creed, Mary Stroud, Fleur Dunsford, Vera Dawe, Eva Creed, Mary Cox, Doreen Gray.*

A View of Melplash

Melplash, meaning millpool, was mentioned in the Domesday Survey and at times shared the same ownership as Mapperton, which has a common boundary.

Melplash Court

Melplash Court took shape in the reign of Henry VI or earlier when a family called de Melplash held the lands. The Mores of Marnhull succeeded, and in Henry VIII's reign it passed from Sir Thomas More to a younger son of the Marquis of Winchester. The story goes that as Sheriff of Dorset, Sir Thomas More one day elected to throw open the gaol at Dorchester to release all the prisoners. He was arraigned for this light-hearted behaviour, and his pardon was procured by the Marquis of Winchester, Lord Paulet, but the price of the pardon was the hand of Sir Thomas More's daughter in marriage for Lord Paulet's second son.

The house was rebuilt early in the seventeenth century, and a further wing added later in the same century. The former west wing was largely destroyed at some uncertain time and was replaced by the existing west wing in 1922. Two overmantels bearing the arms of James I and of Paulet that were originally there were removed to Mapperton House in 1907. There is a circular stone pigeon house that was probably built in the seventeenth century. The house had a chapel, possibly originally a Roman Catholic chapel associated with the Paulets, as Thomas Paulet and his wife Elizabeth were later cited as recusants at Netherbury. The whereabouts of the chapel is today something of a mystery.

Hinknowle, c.1900.

The historian Hutchins mentions that there was a small building adjoining the back of the house called the Chapel. In the sale particulars of 1945 it refers to a chapel opening out of a corner of the drawing-room and extending beyond the front of the house. This may be the one indicated on the 1903 OS map. Another source mentions the clearing of a lumber from a room 'which was used as a chapel'. It may be that this variation reflects the necessity for concealment of Roman Catholic places of worship from the sixteenth century onwards, given that many members of the owners' families were of this religion.

Melplash Court was lent to St Dunstan's, the charity for the blind, by the then owners Mr and Mrs Ruxton during the Second World War. It was used as a convalescent home and also for the charity's permanent invalids evacuated from London and the South East. The graves of those who died there may be seen in Melplash churchyard. A map in the church gives their names and the position of the graves. The whole estate was sold in 1945 with the understanding that the tenancy of St Dunstan's was to continue 'until the end of the war with the German Reich takes place', and in July of that year St Dunstan's moved back to the South East.

Melplash, as an ecclesiastical parish, was taken from Netherbury, North Poorton and Powerstock in 1847. The parish includes the hamlets of Hinknowle, Loscombe, and Oxbridge. Hinknowle belongs to the Best family. The current cider orchards were planted over quite a long period to the present day. There was a big fire at Hinknowle in 1991 and much of the back of the house had to be rebuilt.

Melplash appears to have originally belonged to the Court but the estate had been broken up by the time of the separation of the parish. The reasons for the formation of the parish were that flax growing and the associated industry were expected to expand and Melplash was considered a good site. In fact that expansion never occurred.

'Salvation, Education and Damnation'

James Bandinel financed the building of the church. He was the Senior Foreign Office translator and the owner of Mount Cottage in Oxbridge Lane, but he

One of the St Dunstan's gravestones. Garnet Smith, died 20 May 1945.

Above: *A portrait of Mr Bandinel, which now hangs in the vestry of the church.*

Below: *Inside Christ Church, Melplash, 1922. The nave became a badminton court in 1975.*

lived in Bristol and died of cholera in 1849. He gave the money in memory of his father, the Revd Dr James Bandinel vicar of Netherbury, because he considered that Melplash was too far from Netherbury for the vicar to give proper attention to the sick and the poor.

The church was built 1845–46 in the early Norman style to the designs of Benjamin Ferrey and could seat 300 – one report suggested 1,000, but that seems to be an exaggeration. An example of the Norman Revival, it is a fine building in cruciform shape with an impressive central crossing. In 1975 the decision was taken to bring this magnificent but over-large building into community use. A glass screen was installed to divide the building, and the old nave, now stripped of its pews, is used for social functions, meetings and badminton. The east side of the church is used regularly for worship with the altar now standing in the north transept.

In 1882 a vast manuscript was presented to the Royal Astronomical Society in Piccadilly, London, which included hundreds of calculations and drawings of eclipses of the moon and every eclipse of the sun from England for eight centuries (700–2500AD). The author was the vicar of Melplash from 1881 to 1905, Revd Samuel Johnson, an amateur astronomer.

The pulpit in the church, designed by H.W. Crickmay and carved by W.E. Micklewight, was dedicated on 6 June 1921 to the memory of the men who died and to those who served in the First World War. The men of Melplash who gave their lives in this conflict are recorded in the village's Commonplace Book: Charles Crew, whose family home was the wagon works and who became an assistant schoolmaster in Shaftesbury, died of cholera in Iraq; Arthur Davies, aged 21, of Crooked Oak Cottages was listed as missing in France; Alfred Harp, a twine worker at Slape Mills who lived at Oxbridge was wounded, made a prisoner of war and died in Germany; Frederick Bulteel died of pneumonia in a French hospital in 1918; Alfred Dunham, whose home was Lower Elwell Farm and who was a butcher in Bridport, is believed to have died a prisoner of war in Germany towards the end of the war.

The school, built in the gabled Tudor style, was partially financed by Mr Bandinel and opened in 1849. Before the Second World War the school at Melplash had 30–40 children with two lady teachers, the headmistress, Miss Newman, who lived at the school and the infant teacher, Miss Cousins, who lived at the Post Office.

Melplash Agricultural Society was formed in 1847. The annual show expanded to include cattle, cart horses, ridden horses and horse jumping and by 1871 the show site left Melplash to alternate between various sites in Beaminster and Bridport.

F.J. Legg outside his home at Melplash, c.1910-20.

In 1867 the following trades and businesses were to be found in Melplash: baker, iron founder, a shop, two shoemakers, wheelwright, carpenter, machine proprietor, carrier, butcher, miller, nurseryman, carriage builder, 13 farmers, a farm bailiff and a Post Office.

The present main road between Beaminster and Bridport is almost wholly a turnpike creation. In earlier times the way between the two towns followed the Brit valley. The earliest turnpike also followed this route. A more satisfactory route was created by using lengths of two old roads, one from Bradpole to Melplash by Mangerton Lane, and the other from Netherbury to Melplash and Powerstock. This road probably dates from about 1765. As Melplash village was by this time on a new main route its status, no doubt, increased. Was this one of the reasons why the decision was taken to build a brand new church there in 1846?

A garage, at the time of writing being converted into houses, was a carriage and wagon works for many years, firstly belonging to the Trevett family, predecessors of Rex Trevett the Bridport musician who died recently, and then to the Cousins. The Post Office and shop were originally in the cottages by the garage that is near the entrance to Melplash Farm. The shop was in the cottage by the garage buildings, and the Post Office in the middle cottage. The Crews built a new house and blacksmith's shop between the lane leading to Hinknowle and the lane leading to West Milton. The blacksmith's was a shed at the back while the Post Office and shop were in the house at the front and run by Mrs Crew. Austin Ashford ran the Post Office and shop after the Crews but it eventually closed on 4 November 1981.

The church, school and the Half Moon Inn are next door to one another and are known locally as 'Salvation, Education and Damnation'!

The church, the school and the Half Moon Inn, known locally as 'Salvation, Education and Damnation'.

The rectory in 1908 at Camesworth. The rector is the Revd R.H. Gundry.

THE BOOK OF BEAMINSTER

Melplash School, 1902. Left to right, back row: Sam Marsh, Harry Marsh, Edward Wallbridge, Richard Travers, Ernest Caddy, Mrs Townsend (headmistress), Lill Couzens (teacher), Willie Dunham, Alfred Loveridge, Wilfred Gill, Ernest Read; middle row: ? Loveridge, John Ford, Nat Hawker, Herbert Samways, Harry? Marsh, Harry Read, Reggie Fraggie (with headmistress), ? Loveridge, Ned Scaddens; front row: John Read, W. Crew. Bertie Gulham, Frederick Samways, Edgar Crabb, Albert Derby, Willoughby Travers, ? Samways.

Choir outing to Bournemouth, 4 July 1921.

Top: *Horse and cart near cottages, c.1925. Two of the cottages became derelict during the Second World War and were demolished.*

Above: *Robert and Thirza Watts(the elderly couple in the middle) outside their cottage, c.1910.*

Right: *Melplash Court Farm, 1911.*

The Beaminster Union Workhouse, c.1910-20.

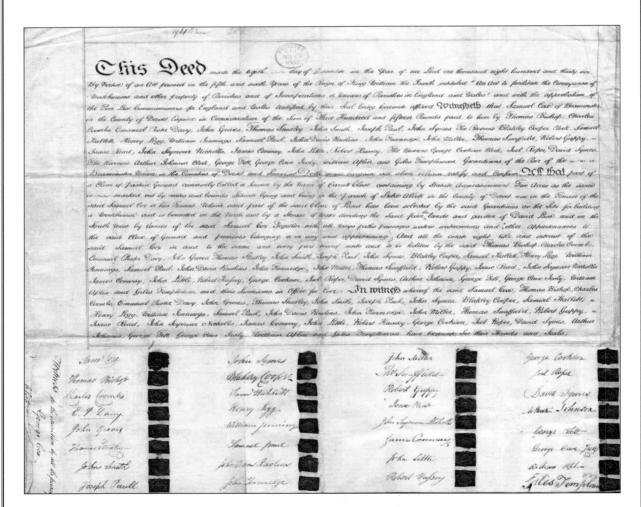

Signatories to the deed for the purchase of land for the Union Workhouse, 1836.

Chapter 7

The Deserving Poor

When old age, unemployment, sickness or death of the breadwinner meant there was no money to put food on the family table or to pay for a roof over the family's heads, 'going on the parish' was often the only solution. The words 'being sent to the workhouse' struck fear into the hearts of people. Before 1834 each parish was responsible for the care of its own poor, either by providing a small allowance or a place in a poor house. The local ratepayers had a financial commitment to pay a poor rate, based on the value of their property, which was collected by an overseer for the poor. Charities might also give some financial support or a last home in an almshouse for an aged pauper. Because paupers were a financial burden on the ratepayers there were active measures taken to send 'outsiders' back to their own parish. Illegitimate children were considered to belong to the parish where they were born so great efforts were made to off-load responsibility. This could go as far as dumping a very pregnant vagrant girl into a ditch across the parish boundary to ensure the baby was born in the neighbouring parish.

Beaminster's first poor house was endowed by Gilbert Adams and built in 1626 in the hamlet of Loscombe. It was rebuilt in 1737 and received inmates for nearly a hundred years. In 1739 it was decided to rebuild the Gilbert Adams almshouses in Beaminster's East Street 'so as to make it capable and fitt to receive the poor of the parish'. In 1748 poor rates were still being collected for 'furnishing, repairing and compleating the workhouse'. The building burnt down in 1766 and was rebuilt, this time with a slate roof instead of thatch. By 1822 additional rooms had been built including a governor's parlour and a schoolroom.

In the eighteenth century it was the intention that workhouses should pay for themselves, although this rarely happened, but in Dorset both Beaminster and Broadwindsor were the most successful in this regard.

Cloth and leather were bought in for inmates to make their own clothes, sheets, blankets and shoes. They gardened to produce vegetables and kept pigs for bacon. Spinning generated income until the greater use of water-powered mills caused a downturn in the need for work done by hand. For a few years from 1818 there was a 'knitting school' in the Beaminster workhouse where children knitted socks and stockings for the inmates and to be sold outside. Some of the able-bodied children were apprenticed as farm labourers or domestic servants. Assisted emigration to the colonies was another way of reducing the need for long-term support. In 1850 the Beaminster Emigration Account paid for Jane Frampton's passage to Adelaide, Australia as well as supplying some cash, her fare to Plymouth, a chest, a new outfit of clothes and the cost of redeeming her own clothes from a pawnbroker.

The Poor Law Amendment Act of 1834 established Boards of Guardians to take charge of the local administration of poor relief and many of the Beaminster's first Board of Guardians were Nonconformist Congregationalists. In Dorset 12 Unions were formed, Beaminster being the last in 1836. The Beaminster Union covered 26 parishes including Beaminster, Bettiscombe, Broadwindsor, Chedington, East and West Chelborough, Corscombe, Evershot, Halstock, Hooke, Mapperton, Marshwood, Melbury Osmund, Melbury Sampford, Mosterton, Netherbury, South Perrott, Pilsdon, Poorstock, North Poorton, Rampisham, Stoke Abbott, Wraxall, as well as Misterton and Seaborough in Somerset. A new Beaminster Union Workhouse was built at Stoke Water, just over a mile from the town in the parish of Stoke Abbott, to accommodate paupers from all these parishes and to replace the small parish workhouses. The land was bought for £315 and the building was based on a modified version of a standard Y-shaped workhouse design. Built by Richard Warr of Beaminster at a cost of £4,120 it opened in June 1838 with sufficient accommodation for 230 inmates. The first master and matron were Mr and Mrs Guppy; other appointments that year were Richard Whitty as porter, John Cox as schoolmaster and Sarah Hayward as schoolmistress.

Life in the workhouse was hard and strict rules applied which, if broken, resulted in harsh penalties. For example the Pauper Offence Book records that in 1842 Sarah Rowe was locked up for 24 hours on bread and water for being noisy and swearing; in 1843 James Park deserted by getting over the wall and was to be whipped; and the following year Isaac Hallett was sent to prison for two months of hard labour for breaking a window! The original building included a 'small dark dungeon' but this was later abolished.

Orphans and those termed 'imbeciles' also ended up in the workhouse. There were separate wards for men, women and children, with married couples and families being segregated. Inmates had to wear uniforms. They were expected to work hard and this included preparing food, garden work, cleaning and laundry, bakehouse work and carpentry as well as

The girls of the Workhouse, 1870.

The boys of the Workhouse, 1870.

oakum picking (unravelling tarred rope to reclaim the fibres) and working in the tailor's shop. Children had their lessons in the workhouse schoolrooms. In 1868 the schoolmaster Thomas Beale taught the boys to play the fife and established the 'Union Fife and Drum Band'. This was popular with both the inmates and the townsfolk and the band would often parade down to Beaminster; in 1869 they played at Parnham at the church Sunday School treat.

Local tradesmen tendered to supply the workhouse with bread, meat, cheese and flour. In December 1839 the Board of Guardians ordered that the inmates 'have plum pudding and strong beer on Christmas day' but generally their diet was meagre as this record of 1842 shows:

	Foodstuff	Men	Women
Breakfast			
	Bread	6oz (175g)	5oz (150g)
	Gruel	1½ pints	1½ pints
Dinner			
Sunday:	Suet or Rice Pudding	16oz (450g)	14oz (400g)
Monday:	Pork	4oz (110g)	3oz (75g)
	Potatoes	2lbs (900g)	2lbs (900g)
Tuesday:	Potatoes	2lbs (900g)	2lbs (900g)
	Bread	4oz (110g)	3 oz (110g)
Wednesday:	Pea Soup	1½ pints	1½ pints
Thursday:	Potatoes	2½lbs (1125g)	2lbs (900g)
Friday:	Bread	6oz (175g)	5oz (150g)
	Cheese	2oz (50g)	2oz (50g)
Saturday:	Meal Soup	1½ pints	1½ pints
	Bread	6oz (175g)	5oz (150g)

Unsurprisingly perhaps, there were complaints – for example, on 26 December 1843 the male inmates petitioned for more food.

In 1849 the Union Workhouse had extra wings added and a second story was built in 1863. In 1864 Vagrants' Wards were erected, providing accommodation for 16 men and three women. In 1907 two rooms were converted to form a chapel for the inmates. By 1912, when the workhouse became officially known as Beaminster Poor Law Institution, it was being used primarily as a district infirmary. Local people still recall men who were 'on the tramp' coming through the town on their way to 'the Union'. In 1930 the building became the Beaminster Public Assistance Institution and during the Second World War it was used for military rehabilitation. Later uses as an infirmary and an old people's residence saw Stoke Water House sold and turned into private dwellings.

Above: *Children from the Union Workhouse in Stoke Abbott, c.1906.*

Right: *The memorial tablet in Stoke Abbott church was unveiled in January 1921 by Sir Henry Peto.*

The Board of Guardians and Rural District Council, 1911/12. Left to right, back row: *C.M. Meech (Relieving Officer), S.M. Wrixon, Freeman Roper JP, W. Mansfield, Revd T. Parker, J.G. Kitson, S.R. Baskett, The Earl of Ilchester JP, Com. Hon. G.F. Digby RN, W. Budden, G. Bugler, G. Johnston, Mrs Andrews (Matron), Nurse Peskett;* middle row: *Sir H. Peto Bart., J.L. Kitson, M. Dawbney, H.S. Studley, S. Gillingham, Revd F. Williams JP (Chairman), W.W. Sampson (Vice-Chairman), J.T. Holloway, A.B. Dawbney, W.J. Major, Frank Bugler (Assistant Clerk), T.D. Andrews (Master of the Union Workhouse);* front row: *C.C. Hann (Inspector of Nuisances), F.G. Wakely (Surveyor of Highways), J.M. Meech (Relieving Officer), F.H. Studley, Canon J. Pulliblank, T.B. Hardy, E. Masters, B. Bussell, W.P. Stephens (Porter), S.R. Meech (Master's Assistant).*

Top: *Stoke Water House, taken in 1967; it has been converted to private dwellings.*

Above: *The front façade of the old workhouse, c.2001.*

Left: *Chris Etherington, who at the time of writing lives in the old workhouse, has visited local schools with the Museum's History Team playing the part of Master of the Workhouse.*

A Glimpse of Mosterton

Lying in the valley of the River Axe, straddling the A3066 that runs from Beaminster to Crewkerne and close to the Somerset border is the village of Mosterton. The Domesday Survey records that:

Richard of Reviers holds Mortestorne. Aelmer held it before 1066. It paid taxes for 6 hides. Land for 5 ploughs. In lordship 2 ploughs; 5 slaves; 8 villagers and 5 smallholders with 3 ploughs. A mill which pays 7s.6d.; meadow, 30 acres; woodland, 1 league long and ½ league wide. The value was and is £12.

The name Mosterton is believed to be of Saxon origin. Mort was a man's name in Old English and the village's earliest name probably meant 'Mort's thorn tree'. The village has been variously recorded as Mortestorne (1086), Mortesthorne (1209), Morteshorn (1298), Motreston (1354), Mottesthorn (1428), Musterton (1431) and Mosterne alias Mosterton (1654). Mosterton is not to be confused with the similarly-named village of Misterton which lies only a short distance away across the border in Somerset.

St Mary's Chapel

Remarkably few archeological remains have been found in the village itself. The site of St Mary's Chapel forms the only medieval feature. This small chapel was originally sited on the north side of the parish, on the opposite side of the road near to where Chapel Court Farm now stands. Hutchins described it as 'a small building containing nothing worthy of notice'. It was a chapel of ease to the church at South Perrott, which was where the villagers were buried, their coffins being carried along Bows Lane. It must have been a nightmare journey for the pallbearers along a rutted and muddy route. Eventually burials took place in Mosterton.

In a 'little sketch' about the Hood family of Mosterton and South Perrott written by Revd R. Grosvenor Bartelot we are told that John Hoode of Mosterton had six children, Richard, Tremor, Alexander, John, Honor and Joane baptised between 1609 and 1620; the youngest, Joane, died aged 13. It was Tremor Hood who raised the fortunes of the family and he that was 'laid to rest

St Mary's Church, Mosterton.

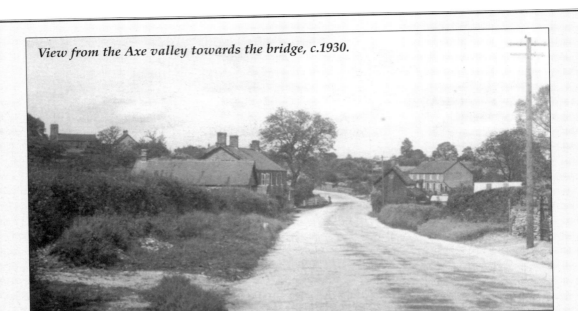

View from the Axe valley towards the bridge, c.1930.

Mosterton School, 1918. Left to right, back row: M. Loveless, A. Hawker, M. Hawker, P. White, R. Lewis, D. Curtis, V. Rogers, R. Case, L. Hutchings?, E. Legg, D. Collier; middle row: D. Bishop, D. Diment, O. Ireland, E. Hawker, O. Brunt, G. Ireland, ? Bussel, ? Bussel, W. Larcombe; front row: S. Legg, J. Norris, E. Ireland, I. Brunt, L. Bishop, E. Hawker, L. Legg, S. Diment, E. Hutchings, B. Larcombe.

The village policemen and others outside the New Inn, c.1910.

The New Inn, now named the Admiral Hood, before the fire on 5 November 1955.

Wedding picture of Robert Roussell, aged 83, with his bride, Mary Ann Wakely, c.1910.

in the little Church at Chapel Court, Mosterton, which has long since passed away.' The grave of Elizabeth Hood who died in 1745 is reputedly in the old chapel yard.

A silver chalice and paten of an 'unusual design' was given in the early-eighteenth century. The engraving around the bowl reads 'Thomas Sandiford of Mosterton, Church Worden. Anno Domini 1714' and although not hallmarked it is considered to be of that period. The surname Sandiford can be found in parish registers of that time. The old chapel was eventually taken down in 1832.

In the seventeenth century smuggling was commonplace and brandy, landed on the coast to the south, was carried by pony to various distribution points. It is said that the chapel or New Inn were used and in 1669 five smugglers were caught in Chedington Lane and 40 gallons of brandy recovered.

The new church of St Mary's was built about half a mile away from its predecessor and was consecrated in 1833. Built of stone by Ellis Daw of South Perrott, it comprised a chancel, a wide nave, a north porch and a western tower bearing one bell. A west gallery is supported by columns and there is an older font. Interestingly it was an Elias Daw with whom the building agreement was drawn up and there is more research to be done to clear up

the Ellis/Elias conundrum. A recent stained-glass window, described by one writer as 'startling but good' was dedicated by the Archdeacon of Salisbury in 1975. Designed by Geoffrey Robinson and made by Joseph Bell of Bristol it portrays Christ Triumphant above an International Harvester and a Ford tractor pulling a Webb single-seeder drill.

A Wesleyan Methodist chapel opened in 1842 and later a chapel for Plymouth Brethren in 1889 which was active until 1997.

A Living From the Land

For centuries the land fed and clothed the inhabitants of the village. In earlier times there used to be a mill powered by the waters of the River Axe which rises in the hills two miles away. A leat carried the water to the mill. Originally a corn mill and later producing sailcloth, like many Dorset mills it changed its use to whatever commodity was most profitable at the time. John Clay in his 1845 will left his interest in the mill machinery to John Woodcock and Henry Smith of Mosterton. In 1851 John Woodcock, Henry Smith, David Ackerman and his 15-year-old daughter Sarah, Frederick Bartlett, Thomas Bell, Ann and Sarah Rousell, and Philip Stuckey, were amongst six hucklers (or hecklers) who combed flax and 25 mill workers. A fall in population at Mosterton shown in the 1851 census was probably linked to a decline in the hemp and flax trade but the flax mill was operating until at least 1880 and later became a corn mill. The millhouse and attached mill building date from the eighteenth and nineteenth centuries.

The opening of the Horn Hill Tunnel in 1832 significantly eased the transportation of produce to Beaminster and Bridport. A number of carriers soon ran regular services between Crewkerne and Beaminster which meant increased prosperity for Mosterton. By the end of the nineteenth century the main crops grown on the clay soil were wheat, barley, oats, peas, hay and turnips.

Prominent Buildings

The village grew around a crossing point of the River Axe and developed in a ribbon-like fashion along the turnpike road. The most notable buildings in the village are the Manor House and Myrtle Cottage which date from the late-seventeenth century, and Woodstock which dates from about 1700. Southview is an eighteenth-century thatched cottage with stone mullions on Bows Lane which took its name from a Mr Bows who lived at Southview in the mid-nineteenth century.

The Admiral Hood (originally called the New Inn) public house carries a date stone for 1748. On 5 November 1955 the New Inn caught fire – given the date one must ask if fireworks could have been responsible. In 1965 the Village Hall was opened and the BBC's *Any Questions* was broadcast from there in 1967.

Schooling in Mosterton

The earliest reference to a school in Mosterton is in 1818 and a Sunday School in 1846/47. A dame-school was listed in 1870 and one is believed to have been at Myrtle Cottage in the mid-1880s when the population numbered around 380. Later a new, purpose-built school was founded next door for 'children of the deserving poor'. The fund-raising was led by the Revd J. Stroud and on 27 March 1876 25 children were admitted. In the early years one schoolmistress, helped by a monitress, taught as many as 70 children.

During the First World War children were given partial or total exemption from school to help on the land and in the Second World War evacuee children formed a fluctuating population in the school. Electricity came to the school in 1945 and drinking water, previously brought from Beaminster on a daily basis, was connected in the 1960s. In 1976 a new primary school was opened half a mile from the old establishment. The bell from the former school, in its original stone setting, was re-erected on the new site.

Men's Club outing, 1920s.

Village outing, 1927. Left to right, standing on the road: *M. Bloomfield, V. Newberry, D. Curtis.* Those on the charabanc include: *A. Case, H. Hawker, P. Stuckey, P. Brunt, W. Stuckey, W. Rousell, V. Brunt, L. Rousell, M. Brunt, D. Crocker, V. Broomfield, D. Hodder, O. Ireland, T. Edwards, Mrs Bugler, Gladys Bugler, Mr and Mrs R. Bowditch with the Churchill twins, O. Brunt.*

Bob Hawker is by the horse. Left to right in the wagon are: *Reg House, Rose Shiner, Sid Bugler, Oswald House and Fred Irish.*

Mrs D. Cox making camouflage nets during the Second World War.

Some village workers. Left to right, back row: Isaac Legg, Reg Case, Percy Case, Harry Stuckey; front row: ?, Sid Bugler, Stanley Hawker.

Mosterton United Football Club, 1924.

Top: *Mosterton Post Office. Miss M. Willmott, the postmistress, is on the left, c. 1940-50.*

Above: *Enterprise Band., c.1940-50.*

Right: *Ogle lift elevator, c.1930, at Sandiford Farm.*

Whatley Mill, as a private house c.1983.

An old flax factory believed to be situated behind The Walnuts at Prout Bridge, c.1909.

Chapter 8
Markets, Merchants and Makers

In 1284 William de Ewell and Thomas de Rupton were granted a weekly market and a three-day fair each September. Townsfolk, farmers and villagers would have descended on Beaminster's busy medieval market each Thursday to sell and buy livestock, meat, dairy produce and other foodstuffs as well as locally produced cloth, blankets, tools and leather goods. In the fourteenth century many markets fell into disuse but Beaminster's continued and a new Market House was built early in the seventeenth century. The town's inns must have done a roaring trade on market days. The fire of 1684 severely damaged the Market House and butchers' Shambles. In about 1780 a replacement was built in the Square; the north and south walls each had five Ham stone arches under which were butchers' stalls. Beaminster market continued until the middle of the nineteenth century.

Cloth-making and the manufacture of hemp and flax products were the most important industries after agriculture. From earliest times wool has been spun and woven. A trade token depicting a wool-comb was issued by William Conway of Beaminster in 1667. In 1724 Daniel Defoe in *A Tour Through England and Wales* named Beaminster as one of the 'market towns which are principally employ'd in the clothing trade'. The local wool was not of the best quality, so much of it was made into coarser fabric. Fleeces were scoured in local fulling mills; one operated in 1656 at the top of Fleet Street, but the spinning and weaving were done in the workers' homes. In the eighteenth century many people were recorded as clothiers, cloth weavers, wool-combers, serge-weavers and wool-staplers. The industry was still thriving in the early 1800s but from 1824 it fell into decline and by 1842 it was almost extinct.

From medieval times hemp and flax were grown locally, the flax to be woven into linen and the hemp for making rope and cordage. Coarse linen was made for sheets and household use, and also heavier weight cloth needed for bags, grain sacks and cart covers. Ships carried more sail and as merchant and naval fleets expanded so the demand for sailcloth grew. By the late-eighteenth century a large number of Beaminster's population was working in the industry. In 1793 Samuel Cox junr, a manufacturer of sailcloth, employed over 600 people and more than 2,000 men and women were working in the Beaminster trade around this time. In 1830 three water mills were being used for spinning flax into yarn needed for sailcloth. The site of Yarn Barton,

now a car park behind Fleet Street, was once used for bleaching yarn. Men and women were also employed in spinning twine, pack thread, shoe thread and rope, and in net-making. By the mid-1800s these trades too had almost died out.

A good water-supply and access to materials such as waste linen, sailcloth and rope were required for paper-making, another local trade. In the eighteenth century there were two paper mills, one at Whatley and one near Prout Bridge. Interestingly a list of prisoners in London's Fleet prison in 1729 includes William Northam, a paper-maker, late of Beaminster! The first recorded printer in Beaminster, William Oliver, printed the appeal for contributions after the fire of 1781. His sons Isaac and James continued in the trade. Other known printers included William Sherring in 1823 and Edwin Coombs in 1842 whose nephew, Thomas Patten Coombs, also a printer, had the first steam-engine to drive machinery in Beaminster.

Trades, Industries and Retail Outlets

Beaminster was home to a wide range of trades. Ralph Cloud, born in 1663, and his son, also Ralph, born in 1692, made the church clocks for Beaminster, Broadwindsor, Stoke Abbott and Netherbury. The Eveleigh, Drake and Peach families were noted Beaminster clockmakers in the eighteenth and nineteenth centuries. All manner of metal workers, blacksmiths, tinsmiths, cutlers and tool makers provided

William Bishop had a carriage works in Clay Lane, where he also made bee and poultry appliances. L. to R., back row: Edith Bishop, Ethel Maud Bishop, ?; front row: William Bishop, Gertrude Bishop, Eliza Rogers Bishop, c. 1900-10.

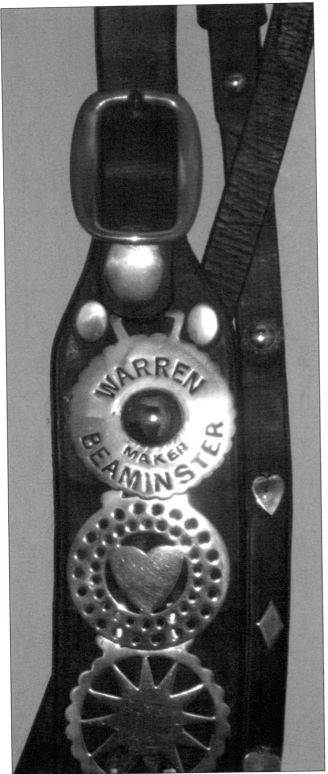

glovers and shoemakers. It is entirely possible that the farm labourer wore boots made from the hides of the very cattle he had tended.

A further use of locally sourced materials was the manufacture of pottery. Much of the town stands on Fuller's Earth clay which, although unsuitable for fine ceramics, was used for the manufacture of bricks and tiles, drainage pipes and pottery. In 1867 Abraham Meech was producing coarse ware at the pottery on Hogshill Street. Robert Chambers was the last potter in the 1880s and the kilns were finally demolished in 1890.

For all household goods the ironmonger was the most important retailer. The firm of A. & E. Toleman was significant in Beaminster. Anthony Toleman was a plumber in the 1830s and by 1855 Anthony and Edward Toleman had become ironmongers as well. They had two large premises in the Square. The ironmonger's shop stood on the corner of Hogshill Street and Fleet Street and stocked an enormous variety of goods. The premises on the opposite corner of Hogshill Street were home to their other trades advertised as 'bell hangers, locksmiths, painters, plumbers, tin plate workers, and agricultural agents' and later 'sanitary engineers'. After 1946 the firm became Colson's.

A. & E. Toleman's premises (left and right), *c.1919.*

Beaminster building contractors from the mid-1800s to the early 1900s included the Chambers, Hann and Symes families. John Warr was based in the Square and his firm built the Union Workhouse in 1836. In 1905 E. Bailey & Son was founded and employed a huge workforce in the 1930s. It is still trading today in Broadwindsor Road. Thomas Crew & Son also employed dozens of men in their heyday.

In the early-nineteenth century Thomas Newman, a plumber and brazier, was the first of a family whose business, over time, embraced all the public utilities as well as domestic electrical and heating engineering. In 1851 Robert Bugler had a sawmill on the River Brit in North Street and was making simple agricultural machines. His sons William and George were timber merchants, cart and wagon builders, wheelwrights and blacksmiths. Francis, William's son, trained as an engineer and today the family firm

A Beaminster horse brass. Warren was a saddler in the Square.

for the population's domestic, agricultural and industrial needs. Wheelwrights and wagon builders, coopers and cabinetmakers, sawyers and carpenters practiced their crafts. Tanning and leather production had been carried out since medieval times and supplied the town's harness-makers and saddlers,

Symes the builders in Fleet Street.

Bugler's stand at the Honiton Show, 1988. Left to right: Ralph Bugler, Dick Down, Brian Brice, John Bugler, Dick Robins

Left: *John Brooks, tailor, c.1900. Born in 1851, one of two sons who was trained by their father, Joshia Brooks, who came to work as a tailor in Beaminster and eventually took over his employer's shop in Hogshill Street.*

of agricultural engineers is still trading in the town.

The town was self-sufficient and had retailers able to provide for everyday needs – maltsters and brewers supplied the inns and also sold from their own premises, often their homes. Other home-based craftspeople included boot and shoemakers, milliners, dressmakers, and tailors. The town's bakers, including Reader and Roberts, obtained flour from the local mills. The bread was made in bake-houses, which were usually attached to the shop from where it was sold. Bread deliveries from hand-carts and horse-drawn carts – and later from bicycles – were made to outlying areas of the town but every small village had its own baker. Beaminster butchers bought livestock on the hoof from the local farmers. The animals grazed in the butchers' fields before being slaughtered. As the Market House fell into disrepair – it was eventually demolished in 1886 – the butchers moved from the Shambles to their own shops. The firm of Frampton & Son can be traced back to at least 1842 when Giles Frampton was a butcher in Fleet Street. In 1880 the shop in the Square was being run by Giles Frampton junr and at the time of writing a butcher's shop is still trading there as Frampton & Son. John Henry Bugler was appren-

A livestock market in the Square early in the twentieth century.

Above: *Frampton's butchers shop, c.1909. Giles Frampton* (far left) *and his two sons Ernest* (second left) *and Charles* (fourth left).

Below: *The Frampton family, c.1905.*

The Square, c.1880–1905.

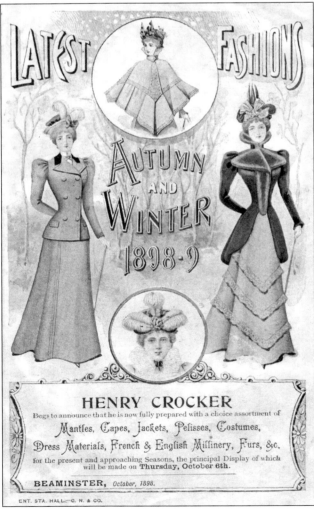

Henry Crocker ran a large draper's shop in the Square.

ticed to Benjamin Froome, a butcher in Hogshill Street, in about 1873. He later had his own butcher's shop in Church Street and his grazing fields were on both sides of Tunnel Road. At the start of the twentieth century Alfred Gibbs was a butcher and cattle dealer at Newtown and Hine Bros in North Street proudly announced, in 1911, 'the only cold storage proprietors & pure ice makers in the district'.

Drapers sold dress materials, household linens, furnishing fabric and haberdashery goods and sewing requisites. As well as selling the materials needed for making garments and household linens drapers also became general outfitters. In 1880 Edwin Coombs' shop was at London House in Hogshill Street but by 1895 had been taken over by Arthur E. Reynolds who traded as a draper and shoe mercer. In 1885 Henry Crocker became the proprietor of a drapery business at Manchester House, now No. 21 the Square, succeeding Henry Virgint who had taken over George Brough's drapery shop there in 1855. Crocker's shop was a large general outfitter which sold men's, women's and children's garments, fabrics and haberdashery, accessories, millinery and footwear. Crocker and Reynolds were the largest of the Beaminster drapers.

Grocers grew in importance as more people became able to afford the increasingly wide range of products which were available. Some grocers were very small concerns run from the front room of the proprietor's home and selling a variety of basic provisions and household goods. The most prominent grocery was Pine's, which traded in Beaminster from 1780 to 1987. The shop moved to its new premises in Fleet Street after a disastrous fire in the Market

Pines the grocers in Fleet Street.

Right: *This shop on the corner of Whitcombe Road was probably owned by Henry Galpin, a baker, confectioner and grocer, c.1885.*

Pines staff, c.1910. Left to right, back row: Turner, ?, Trenchard, Dommett?; front row: Symes, Reggie Pine, Alfred Pine, William Holt, Henry Herbert Hann?

House in 1844. In 1880 Alfred Pine ran the shop which was taken over by Thomas Reginald Pine in the early 1900s and later by Mr Hann. The shop stocked a wide range of grocery provisions as well as wines and spirits, laundry and other household goods, chocolate and cocoa products. It was featured in a television programme made by the BBC when it finally closed after over trading for over 200 years in Beaminster.

The Hine family were grocers and druggists in the town for nearly 135 years. In 1793 Richard Hine bought shop premises in the Square and started his business as a grocer and tea dealer. One son, Benjamin, took over the grocery in 1839 and his youngest son, Philip, was a wine merchant. His eldest son, also Richard, was a druggist. Richard's pharmacy was on the corner of North Street and Fleet Street and his son Alfred was his partner from 1852. In 1880 the pharmacist's shop was moved next door to the grocery (across the Square).

In 1882 Richard, also a chemist, photographer and author of *A History of Beaminster*, took over the shop. He left many photographs of the town and there were also other photographers at this time including Angelina Barrett, who practised from 1885 and her niece Augusta who worked in Beaminster between 1889 and 1911. In 1885 James Dare was in Church Street, V.H. Allen was a printer and photographer in 1919 and William Guppy was a photographer in Fleet Street from 1919 to 1930.

The Post Office was important to the town. In 1851 the postmistress was Frances Frampton in Hogshill Street. Jeremiah Stembridge, a saddler, was the postmaster from 1865, moving the Post Office to Church Street in about 1885. Mrs Jane Stembridge took over in the early 1900s. From about 1913 to the 1960s the Post Office was situated at No. 2 the Square, later moving to No. 18 Hogshill Street where it is today.

There were shops which sold stationery and books, gifts and fancy goods, china and glass. There were hairdressers, cycle agents, thatchers and chimneysweeps, painters and decorators, furniture- and watchmakers, a signwriter and a manufacturer of beehives. There were shops selling sweets and tobacco and newsagents supplied the townsfolk with periodicals and newspapers.

Central to trade and commerce were the banks. In 1842 there were two banks, a branch of William's Bank and a branch of the Bridport Bank, the latter failing in 1847. In 1855 there was only the Dorchester & Dorsetshire Bank but by 1867 the Wilts & Dorset also had an office in the town. In 1872 an impressive

A Beaminster telegraph boy, 1920–30.

Miss Curtis (left) *and Miss Marsh who ran a sweetshop in Swan Lane, a colloquial name for the part of Fleet Street near Yarn Barton approaching the Square. The Swan Inn was once sited here.*

A new bank was built in the Square in 1872. This photograph probably dates from between 1880 and 1900.

new bank building in the Square was home to the Dorsetshire, taken over by the Wilts & Dorset by the 1890s, and then taken over by Lloyds in the twentieth century. These premises are now privately owned. In 1921 the London Joint City & Midland Bank opened in the Square in the building previously the premises of Richard Swatridge, a corn and seed merchant. Still a bank, it is now a branch of HSBC.

Twentieth-century employers included Numatic, who made the iconic Henry vacuum cleaner. Abbot Brown was an engraver and manufacturer of printed plastic signs, whose factory site in Fleet Street was previously occupied by an egg depot. At West Surrey Central Dairy Co. at Prout Bridge, dried milk powder was made. Aplin & Barrett, producers of preservatives for the food industry, took over the site and the company is now owned by Danisco. The most recent employer of significance in the town is Clipper Teas who market Fairtrade and organic products. Their premises are situated on both sides of the Broadwindsor Road. Further along the road is a small business park situated in the old Horn Park Quarry.

The history of Beaminster is inextricably linked to the fortunes of its tradespeople and shopkeepers – as well as serving their customers they served their community as stalwarts of church and chapel, as guardians of the poor, as parish and town councillors; in wartime and peacetime they have always been at the forefront of civic life.

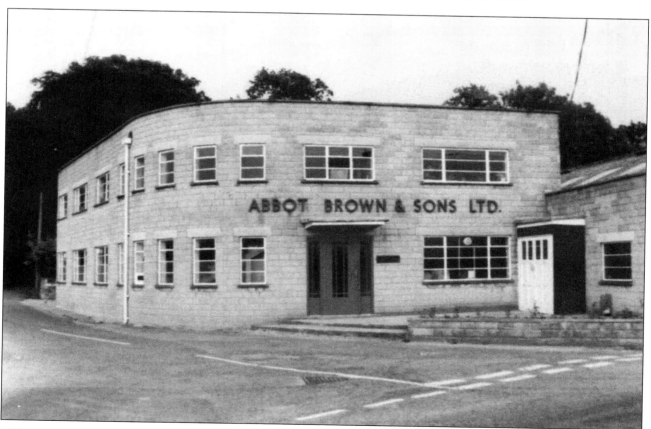

Abbot Brown, c.1983. This factory was closed on 31 October 2004.

West Surrey Central Dairy started the milk factory in Beaminster in 1904. This picture shows the staff and vehicles in about 1920. The chimney is still a feature of the site today.

Aplin and Barrett, producers of milk powder products. The firm was taken over by Danisco.

A Look At Netherbury

The village of Netherbury is 1½ miles south of Beaminster. The River Brit runs through the village to the sea just 6 miles further to the south. It has been a site of human habitation from earliest times and archaeological finds include flint and stone objects dating from the Prehistoric, Mesolithic and Neolithic periods. The name is derived from the Old English *neotherra* and *burh* meaning 'lower fortified place'. It is recorded in Domesday in 1086 as Niderberie, and other variations have included Nutherbir (1226) and Nitherbury (1285). The parish was once one of the largest in Dorset having three prebendaries: Netherbury in Terra or Yondover to the east of the river; Slape to the south of the river and Netherbury in Ecclesia, the largest, containing the village of Netherbury.

Worship at Netherbury

The Church of St Mary the Virgin stands on high ground and is probably not the first to have stood there. It has been suggested that there was once a Saxon church, not necessarily on the same site, and later a Norman one. The font certainly dates from the twelfth century, the nave from the mid-fourteenth century and the chancel from the fifteenth century. The first known vicar of Netherbury and Beaminster was David Stalbridge in the 1300s. In the church is a striking feature, a tomb on which lies the figure of a knight. Dressed in armour, with chainmail at his neck and a sheathed dagger hanging from a studded belt, his helmet is surmounted with a bird – possibly a dove or moor-cock. Local tradition tells that this knight, after defeating another in combat in a nearby field, had his innocence confirmed by a dove settling on his helmet. It is probable, however, that the bird is the crest of the More family who owned Melplash Manor before the reign of Henry VI.

The fifteenth-century tower has six bells dating from 1610 and there is fine carved Elizabethan pulpit. Also of interest is a brass plaque commemorating Admiral Sir Samuel Hood (1762–1814) and his two brothers, the 'Three Gallant Dorset Sailors'. Samuel Hood served with Nelson at Santa Cruz and the Battle of the Nile. One brother, Alexander, sailed with Captain Cook on his second voyage around the world. All three were born in the parish at Kingsland Farm.

Three windows were added in 1946 as a memorial to those who died in the Second World War. The smaller one over the north door was designed by Christopher Webb, the other two by his pupil

Netherbury church.

The Congregational chapel and Post Office.

The original chapel at Waytown, pre-1901.

Francis Skeate. Many are surprised that until 1849 Beaminster Church remained a chapel of ease to Netherbury which was its mother church.

Other places of worship included a Methodist meeting-house recorded in 1796 and a Wesleyan Methodist chapel built in 1828. In Waytown a Congregational chapel was licensed in 1672 and rebuilt in 1901.

The Witch of Netherbury

A local tale relates the story of a witch in the parish. John Walsh of Netherbury was a servant to 'a Popish priest', Robert Drayton. This priest had 'taught him physick and surgery, and much else of a less praiseworthy nature.' After Drayton's death Walsh reappeared in the village. He had with him his master's book 'which had great circles in it, wherein he would set two wax candles and a cross of virgin wax to raise the familiar spirit.' It would appear to him in the form of a grey calf, a brindled dog or a man with cloven feet and Walsh would reward this spirit for its services with a chicken, a cat or a dog.

He was accused of making effigies in wax and clay to cause people to fall ill and also of communing with fairies in a fairy hut on a high hill. Taken before the Commissary of the Bishop of

Exeter in August 1566 he said that there were three kinds of fairies, the black, the white and the green, 'of which black be the worst'. He complained that the Constable of Crewkerne had confiscated his book and he was powerless without it. Sadly there is no record of what happened to John Walsh.

Education

There was a school in Netherbury in 1546. It is generally accepted that it was in existence from the fifteenth century, although claims that it was founded in 1460 are unsubstantiated. It was endowed with the profits of two farms, purchased with funds provided by an unknown benefactor, known as Broadnam and Paradise in the manor of Slape and provided free education for boys. In 1759, when considering the appointment of a new schoolmaster, the Vestry meeting declared that

> ... the Schoolmaster of the said School... always shall well and diligently Teach and Instruct all such Boys... in Reading, Writing, Arithmetic and Latin and Greek... [and] in their Duties of Religion according to the Church of England by the Law Established...

In 1830 the old school premises had become dilapidated and a house situated near the church was chosen for the use of the schoolmaster and a new schoolroom for 60 boys was built at the cost of about £100.

Following the Endowed Schools Act of 1869 control of Netherbury Grammar School was lost by the Netherbury Vestry under a plan to establish a new middle school to serve the wider rural community. The parishioners were unhappy to lose their grammar school but in 1881 it finally joined with Beaminster's Tucker Free School to become Netherbury & Beaminster Grammar School, located in the nearby town.

In 1842 a school for girls and infants was established in the village and in 1863/4 a new National School was built which also admitted boys. Children were very much involved in agriculture and the school log-book of the time records children absent for potato and apple picking, haymaking, gleaning and collecting acorns for pigs. By 1878 pupil numbers had increased to the extent that the school had to be enlarged. It closed in 1974 and these days Netherbury children travel to the modernised primary school at Salway Ash.

Agriculture in Netherbury

Netherbury is a place of fertile land and ample water. John Leland, who visited the area in 1546, thought it had the best corn, pasture and woodland in Dorset. Hutchins, in his *History of Dorset*

Netherbury Bridge, c. 1895-1900. The task of filling the oil-lamp was once performed by George Watts.

first published in 1774 recorded its arable, sheep pasture and dairy grounds, its cider orchards, and its stone quarries providing lime for burning to improve the land which 'annually produce great quantities of potatoes, flax and hemp'. A county order of 1791 names those responsible for the upkeep of bridges listing over 25 bridges, the largest number of any local parish.

Flax and hemp were grown extensively as raw materials for the manufacture of rope and twine which was centred on Bridport and for the production of sailcloth and linen. Flax could be grown by smallholders renting a field and growing and harvesting their crop. They would strip the plants,

rot or 'ret' the fibres in streams or ponds, boil out the unwanted material and then comb out or 'heckle' the strands which would then be spun by cottagers in their own homes.

Later, water-powered mills, sometimes originally grist or corn mills, took over flax and tow spinning. By 1851 the census shows 73 people in the village, excluding the flax growers and mill owners, in flax-related occupations and 40 women and children engaged in netmaking and twine braiding at home, with Clenham Mill employing 42 workers and Slape Mill 24 people. In the 1880s there were 'two flax and two tow manufactories'. There was a steep decline in the trade in the early 1900s although there

A derelict Clenham Mill. Once a grist mill, it was used for flax and tow spinning in the mid-nineteenth century.

Above: Albert Dowle and his sister, Alice, outside the Brandon Hotel. This carriage could be hired to convey people to the station at Crewkerne or Bridport. Originally a private house, Brandon Villa became an inn c.1901.

Right: Netherbury Post Office, c.1910.

was flax spinning and twine-making at Slape Mill in 1915. The First World War saw a new demand for flax and by 1942 over 100 people, including gangs of Land Girls, were harvesting and processing flax. At Slape Mill 30 Bournemouth school-children were encamped to help with the flax harvest where 'in 1939 there had been derelict walls and but two families of farm-workers.'

Brewing and Boozing

Small-scale brewing of ale and cider for home consumption supplemented the draughts supplied by the local inns which, at various times, included the Queen's Head, the Albion, the Crook Inn at Yondover, the Hare & Hounds at Waytown, and the Star. The Knapp Brewery near Bridge Street was built by William Hoare, the licensee of the New Inn, in 1846 and was sold to Samuel Hine in 1856 and it was then run by his sons James and Henry. By 1860 it had taken over three Bridport public houses as well as holding the licences for the Star Inn and the New Inn in Netherbury. In 1876 it was bought and immediately closed by John Legg who also owned the Old Brewery in Bridport, perhaps because it was unwelcome competition. In 1896 Palmers Brewery took over the premises to use for storage. It was demolished in 1938. The Brandon Hotel, once a private house called Brandon Villa, was a well-known hostelry in the village.

150 Years of Change

In 1841 the population was 2,162 and in 1851 the village was self-sufficient with public houses and beer sellers; retailers of meat, bread, groceries, boots and shoes, and drapery; as well as carpenters and builders, a wheelwright, basket-, barrel- and rake-makers, as well as a blacksmith. By 1870 the population had fallen to 1,600, and by 1948 to about 600. In 2007 there is no shop and no inn.

Major Gollop of Strode Manor, a writer of popular patriotic and temperance songs. He was taken ill and died at a local concert where he was performing his rousing pieces.

A general view of the village.

The consecration of the war memorial in the churchyard, 1921.

Slape Manor, c.1908.

Chapter 9
The Steep Climb

Beaminster is surrounded by hills on which are the remains of Iron Age forts at Pilsdon Pen, Lewesdon, Lamberts Castle, Coneys Castle, and further away at Eggardon. These hill-forts were joined by tracks to a ridgeway route linked to the Great Ridgeway. These tracks would have been used when travelling any great distance with goods carried by people and by oxen.

The Romans arrived in the first century AD. The Second Legion had a slow advance from Wareham to Exeter. Waddon Hill near Stoke Abbott was a Roman garrison fort. Many of the Roman tracks have now become roads and the main roads from Dorchester to Ilchester and from Dorchester to Axminster originate from this occupation. Several villages, such as Halstock, had villas, or Romano-British farms that would have supplied produce to the larger towns such as Ilchester and Dorchester. After the Romans left many of the roads fell into disrepair for some centuries.

The Road Network Spreads

Bridport in medieval times was a prominent centre of commerce, particularly for rope and net. There were probably links either side of the River Brit from Bridport to Beaminster. Beaminster may have been the inland distribution head with tracks to Crewkerne, South Perrott, Corscombe and Halstock.

By the late-sixteenth century the economy was expanding due to the increase in foreign and internal trade. In addition, well-to-do people were also travelling around the country either on horse back or in coaches. Beaminster with its large escarpment did not provide a practicable route from Bridport. The carts went through Salway Ash, Broadwindsor and up the more gradual slope towards Crewkerne. The ways were stony, narrow and muddy and the heavy wagons with their large wheels churned up the surfaces. The Highways Act of 1555 laid the main responsibility for roads on the parishes through which they passed. On four or six days every year every person holding land to a certain value who kept horses or a plough had to send two men to work on the roads. There were also highway surveyors or waywardens and in 1670 the surveyors for Beaminster were George Beere and John Gudge of Axnoller; in 1691 the waywarden, John Herne, was paid for rebuilding Hams Bridge.

By the eighteenth century Beaminster hemp and flax trades, together with paper-making, printing, potteries, metalworking, clock-making, tanning,

malting and brewing all required a lot of transport and travel. In the eighteenth and nineteenth centuries the advent of turnpikes improved the road system. The Bridport Turnpike Trust had built the road from Bridport, through Melplash to Beaminster. In 1754 a meeting was held at the White Hart in Beaminster to discuss the location of the turnpike gates. At the Beaminster end it was to be between 'Parnham Stile and Mr Baruch Fox's dwelling house' and was later called the Beaminster South Gate. By 1765 the Bridport to Beaminster road became the Bridport Second District.

The introduction of turnpikes and tolls improved the major roads, but the minor roads in the valleys were '… crooked, narrow, numerous and full of sloughs'. There

Top: *A local carter with two members of his family at Melplash.*

Middle: *A cart loaded with wicker hampers.*

Bottom: *This van probably went to the villages delivering household goods, as shown on the side, c.1930.*

Above: *The toll-house north of the Horn Hill tunnel. The toll-house keeper was responsible for lighting the lamps in the tunnel.*

Right: *Southgate, the toll-house and gate at the south end of Beaminster.*

Right: *The tunnel at Horn Hill is the only pre-railway road tunnel still in use in England. This photograph was probably taken in about 1860.*

Above: *The coach is outside the White Hart Inn in Beaminster, a former coaching inn. The front horse may have been added for the climb up the hill to the tunnel and would then have been unhitched and used as a brake horse for the next carriage coming down the hill.*

Left: *Sunday School outing leaving Beaminster from outside the Red Lion. The photograph was taken c.1905.*

were regular coaches, carriers and wagons to and from Beaminster. For example in 1793 Russell's wagon from Exeter to London passed through every Thursday. In 1842 the carriers Whitmarsh & Co. were making three journeys a week to Yeovil and London, and three to Ilminster and Bristol.

The road surfaces were maintained, eventually laid with macadam, but the hill north from Beaminster still posed a problem. In 1830 the Bridport Second Turnpike Trust launched an appeal for money to build a tunnel through Horn Hill for the northbound route from Beaminster. Loans were advanced by 45 local firms and individuals, ranging from £2,000 to £50, the total being nearly £12,000. The tunnel engineer, Michael Lane, was recommended by Marc Brunel, father of Isambard Kingdom Brunel. He had been a bricklayer for the Rotherhithe Tunnel designed by the Brunels, and he later went on to become the Chief Engineer of the Great Western Railway.

The tunnel was completed in 1832, after some difficulties due to the geology and with one fatality, William Aplin, a labourer. The opening was a grand event on 29 June 1832 with a 21-gun salute fired on Horn Hill at 8 o'clock. At 10a.m. a procession, nearly half a mile long, was led by the Bridport and Beaminster bands followed by the Bridport and Taunton Mail Coach, and the carpenters, masons and other tradesmen each bearing the tools of their trade. Some 9,000 people attended the opening by Giles Russell of Beaminster, the main contributor to the tunnel fund.

The tunnel is 106 metres long. It is one of only three road tunnels constructed before the railways, the others being at Charmouth (1832 by the same engineer), and Reigate (1823). The Beaminster tunnel is the only one still in use for daily traffic. Coaches and more of the heavier traffic now come through Beaminster for a more direct route to and from Bridport.

The road from Beaminster to Holywell, the other side of Evershot, became the responsibility of the Maiden Newton Trust set up in 1778. The road from Beaminster to Toller Down Gate is largely a creation of the turnpike trust. At one end was a toll-house at Toller Down Gate and at the other was the last cottage on the left going out of Beaminster on Whitcombe Road. There was also a turnpike road from Bridport through Salway Ash to Broadwindsor.

Trains amd Buses

There were plans for potential railways from Crewkerne or Chard to Beaminster of standard gauge and one narrow gauge, but none came to fruition. The nearest station to Beaminster is Crewkerne and a Beaminster to Crewkerne Station horse-omnibus service was inaugurated in 1860. In 1914 Cecil Hann of the Beaminster Garage Co. started a service by motor brake carrying 14 passengers

between Bridport, Beaminster and Crewkerne.

Public transport was not without its perils. In September 1921 a motor bus operated by the National Omnibus Company on the Bridport to Crewkerne run, loaded with passengers, had pulled up outside the Red Lion. After putting on the brake the driver left the vehicle which rolled backwards down Prout Bridge hill. Mrs Snell and her 13-year-old daughter Dora were among the passengers who jumped from the bus. Dora was injured and died later in hospital.

Some village trades made use of the railways. For example, the watercress from Hooke went by railway each day to London, being served at the Ritz the next day. The local sawmills also tended to use this faster mode of transport, using the route either through Maiden Newton or Crewkerne. The Maiden Newton to Bridport line was a late closure under Lord Beeching's axing of branch lines in the 1960s and 1970s.

The hire of horse-drawn vehicles for outings was popular even during the First World War, as a tripper to West Bay recalled:

We set off early taking all our food, picnicked on the beach, often lighting fires from driftwood to boil a kettle of tea. On the homeward journey the older children had to get out and walk up hills, and push to help the horse, especially going up Crooked Oak, Melplash.

Motorcars, lorries and buses in the early days created a lot of noise and dust. Road repairs continued to be a source of contention in Beaminster right up 1928. Who was to pay? How was the money to be raised? What equipment should be bought? Should contractors be used? Things have not really changed!

This crash occurred at Dibberford Farm on the road to Mosterton north of the tunnel. Mr Arthur Nalder Stephens of Haddon House, Bridport was the owner of this 60 hp Napier phaeton in green and black, weighing 36 cwt. It was first registered on 29 March 1910. It was re-registered on 3 October 1919 to a Mr Campbell Wilcookson of No. 35 Cheapside, London as a 39½ cwt. laundaulette white, with green lines. Presumably it was re-built after the accident!

Charabanc outing from the Blue Ball at Salway Ash. The charabanc was first registered in 1922.

Above: *Inside Perry and Perry's workshop on Broadwindsor Road, Beaminster.*

Below: *Lorry belonging to Perry and Perry.*

Motorbike and sidecar broken down on the flooded road from Stoke Abbott to Beaminster. The motorbike was a Triumph, first registered to C. Smith of Stoke Abbott in 1926.

Road repairs in Beaminster in 1924.

Prout Bridge builders yard owned by the Hann family, with wagons upturned and doorways and windows damaged after the 1894 flood.

Hann's Garage in 1912. The three people with the bicycles are Bill Tuck, Tom Ackerman and Edward Guppy.

This photograph, c.1920, was taken by W.H. Guppy. Left to right: Arthur Hann? (in rear car), ? Wildren (standing to the right of the car), Harold Edwards (in the arch), Albert Hann (in front car). The cars, left to right, are possibly a 6 cylinder Lanchester Sporting 60, and a 1913 American RCH (Robert Craig Hupp) 22 hp tourer with Dorset trade plates.

Hann's Garage, c.1938, by which time there were petrol pumps.

I cannot in any way patronise any such affair, in fact I am prejudiced against such obstacles on the public highways having had on various occasions narrow escapes (probably from serious injury) by having my horse run into by persons mounted on what in my opinion is an unsightly machine.

Thomas Macey, the hairdresser at No. 18 Hogshill Street, hired out bicycles and was a cycle agent. For many people bicycles were the only affordable means of transport. Later came motorcycles, which were sold by Beaminster Garage. A sidecar, although difficult to control, meant the wife and sometimes the family could be taken too.

Two Wheels

Bicycles had also become popular and could be hired or purchased in Beaminster from about 1899. A Beaminster Cycle Club had been set up in 1880 and Mr Coombs rode in front with a warning bugle! Peter Meech, a local dignitary, sent the following response after receiving a copy of the club rules:

The Impact of Traffic on the Town

Traffic and traffic signs have transformed the appearance of the Square and the town. It is only after 2000 that any Beaminster resident has been known to arrive by helicopter!

Above: *The car is a Quadrant 7 hp Tri-car that was manufactured in 1907. It was a tricycle with the two wheels at the front and the engine mounted in between them. The car shown in the photograph is much modified from the original design and may have a homemade body. It was registered on 9 February 1914 to George Edward Martin at Bridgend in Wales. The registration was cancelled and declared void by July 1914. Later it was registered to Albert Henry Martin in Beaminster. Is this the owner with his dog?*

'Yummy' and 'Cissy' Pim in Dr Pim's car outside the Red Lion.

A 1927 Chevrolet at Corscombe owned by Albert Edward Bath who ran the bus service from his shop in Corscombe during the 1920s and '30s. The bus from the village to Yeovil ran four times a week, with a shuttle to East Coker.

Salway Ash: Along the Turnpike Road

Salway Ash (sometimes Salwayash or Solway Ash) is in the civil parish of Netherbury. It is a scattered community with several farm settlements including North Bowood and South Bowood, both of which are mentioned in Domesday. In the thirteenth century Esse, meaning ash, is mentioned, and the village is recorded as Shallways Ash in 1682. There is evidence of much earlier settlement in the area indicated by a Neolithic axe found at Kershay Farm. Many place names suggest Anglo Saxon settlement such as ham (farm), hay and haeg (meaning enclosure).

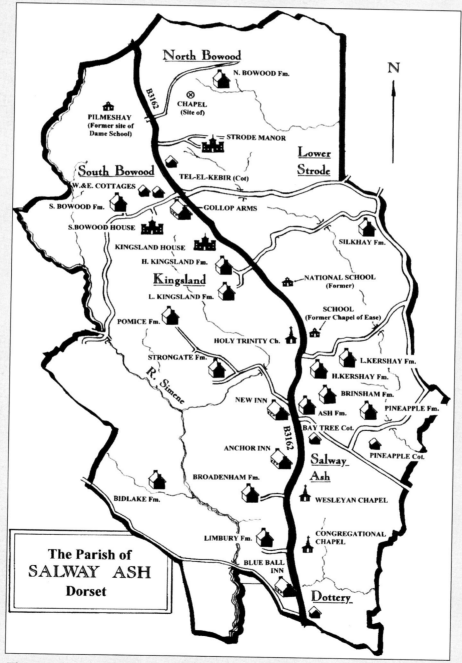

The map shows the scattered settlements of Salway Ash and the names of the farms on which those settlements were based.

Outside the Gardener's Arms at Salway Ash in 1908. These wagons are on the turnpike road that ran between Bridport and Broadwindsor. Mrs Chubb is in the doorway, Mr Chubb by the wheel (he was the publican), Fred and Jack Chubb are in the middle with their grandmother, George Dare is by the wagon with the cider barrel and the carter from North Bowood Farm is by the horses and the wagon with the hurdles.

Many of the farmhouses date from the fourteenth to the seventeenth centuries. In the seventeenth century housing was a problem and houses were often built overnight on wasteland in order to overcome the landowner's control. In March 1639 Thomas Studley erected a cottage at Ash Lane obstructing the highway and the Netherbury constables were ordered to remove it. The court forbade the erection of any cottages in the highway without the special order of the Assizes so by July Thomas Studley was bound over for the removal of the cottage. By March 1640 the court again ordered the demolition of the cottage but Hubert Hussey JP tried to mediate a settlement. By July that year he had done nothing about mediating 'by reason of his earnest occasions otherwise'. He was asked again to examine the matter with a threat of a writ of execution if he failed, empowering the sheriff to demolish the cottage. The records do not tell us how it was resolved!

'There would have been great hardship if the agricultural labourer could not get an honest pint of beer.'

Times were hard and the water was often not fit to drink so alcoholic beverages were generally considered to be a safer alternative. In 1625 Netherbury, of which Salway Ash was a part, was described as a 'Den of Iniquity'! There were at least four inns in Salway Ash. The hamlet of Kingsland and Furley became a resort of the local villains:

They take libertie to themselves to keepe unlicensed Alehouses, and have doiverse disorderlie meetings, where, it is fearde, many stolen goods are consumed to the griefe and loss of manie of their honest neighbours.

The term 'public house' did not come into use until 1850. In the nineteenth century there were five public houses, all on the turnpike road.

The Turnpike

The Bridport and Broadwindsor Turnpike Trust was formed in 1828 with a view to making a turnpike road from the Bridport turnpike at Allington, through Salway Ash to Broadwindsor and Drimpton to join the Crewkerne turnpike. In 1854 the trustees decided that:

The said common public carriage road or King's highway is much out of repair, narrow and incommodious for the passing of cattle and carriages... and should be amended, widened, improved, repaired and made turnpike standard.

A toll-bar existed across Pineapple Lane, with the charges listed as follows:

Pay for every horse or beast drawing a coach, stagecoach, chariot, hearse, landau, chaise or phaeton.
Horse, mule or donkey not drawing 1/-
Horse or beast drawing a wagon, wain or cart 2d.
Drove of oxen or cattle per score 1/6
Drove of calves, swine, sheep or lambs per score 0d.

The turnpike was 9½ miles long.

A Place to Worship

A chapel of ease was erected in 1832 by James Brookland at Coles Ash and this is now the main building of the primary school. Divine services could be held there but funerals and weddings were at Netherbury, for which payment was made. A plot of land opposite was bought in 1879 for £100 to build a new church to replace the chapel of ease. The architects were Crickmay & Sons, for whom Thomas Hardy had worked for some time. The clerk of works appears to have been the vicar, the Revd Gildea, and local workers were employed. The final cost was £2,000 and the church was consecrated by the Bishop of Salisbury in January 1890. Much of the internal work was carried out by local people including carving by Mrs Gundry of Slape, Mrs Grimson of Hatchlands and the Revd Gildea himself. The reredos panel was painted by Miss Hestor Gildea.

William Catton followed his father and trained for the ministry. After being ordained and working in London and Swanage he moved to Netherbury as assistant curate to the Revd Gildea. He lodged with the vicar who had several daughters and a romance developed with the youngest,

Above: *External view of Holy Trinity Church from the churchyard.*

Left: *The Revd William Catton's grave.*

Salway Ash School, 1920.

Angelina, and they became engaged. In 1892 he moved to a curacy at Corfe Castle. Whilst assisting with Holy Communion he became unwell and fell and hit his head on one of the chancel steps. He died a few hours later. He had once indicated that he wished to be buried at Salway Ash and so it was that on 3 August 1892, three weeks before he was due to be married, his funeral took place. His gravestone is in the churchyard and a window is dedicated to his memory.

There was also a Wesleyan Methodist chapel built in 1846 but it has since closed and a Congregational church, built in 1843, was closed in 1940.

It is believed there was once a dame-school at Salway Ash. In 1859 a National School was opened. In 1871, after the Foster Education Act required children to be educated to the age of 11, the old school was too small and the former chapel of ease was converted into a school. The school is still in use today and includes the children from the former schools at Melplash and Netherbury.

Kershay Farm

Kershay Farm may be 'the house with some land and a

Malthouse, some distance from any village, called Kersey' in Elizabeth Ham's mid-eighteenth century diary. She wrote, 'my parents' nearest neighbours were the Hoods'. The well-known family of naval officers had connections with Salway Ash. Sir Samuel Hood was born at Kingsland in 1762. After commanding several frigates between 1788 and 1796 he transferred to HMS *Zealous*, a ship of the line. In 1802 he became Commander-in-Chief of the Leeward Islands. In September 1805 he was seriously wounded in an engagement with the French. He was shot in the right elbow by a musket and had to have his arm amputated. On 1808 he became the Member of Parliament for Bridport. He was created a baronet in 1809 and promoted to Vice-Admiral in 1811, becoming Commander-in-Chief of the East Indies. He died in Madras in 1814 following a high fever.

Salway Ash Today

In 2007 Salway Ash has a number of modern dwellings as well as a new Village Hall, close to the one remaining public house. Pineapple Farm has become a business centre.

Vice Admiral Sir Samuel Hood, born at Kingsland, Salway Ash, 27 November 1762.

Three men and two women in hayfield by a thatched farmhouse, Brinsham Farm, first mentioned in 1340.

A group of children and their teachers outside the Congregational church ready for their outing, c.1920. They are accompanied by Iris Banter on the left and Mrs Giles on the right. The children include: Barbara Thomas, Ted Slade, Marjorie Spencer, Eireen Green, Jack Stone, Philip Shapcott, Lloyd Thomas, ? Russell and one or two of the Giles boys.

Broadenham Farm was first recorded in 1327 although the current building is clearly more modern.

Pineapple Farm in 1936, originally dating from 1662.

Right: *The Blue Ball Inn on fire on a winter morning in 1947 showing the collapsed thatched roof and a number of men who may include Jack Spencer, Fred Roper, Fred Legg, George Parker, Mr Reynish and Mr Lock.*

Practically the whole village and a few others went on this outing to Portsmouth and Southsea in 1946 along with several crates of beer.

Townsend's Fair, 1932. The fair's arrival was eagerly anticipated each year.

Above: *Celebrations in the Square for Queen Victoria's jubilee in 1897.*

Right: *Victoria's diamond jubilee, 1897. The people are standing in front of the police station and the decorated building was a bank.*

Chapter 10
When Work Is Done

In the twenty-first century it is difficult for us to imagine a world without electricity. Until the mid-1900s entertainment was entirely home grown. Adults and children worked hard and for long hours without the luxury of leisure time and so any event which broke up the monotony and drudgery of everyday life was eagerly anticipated.

Beaminster Fair

From medieval times the annual Beaminster Fair allowed for merrymaking and revelry. In 1629 a company giving puppet shows was banned after the constable told the Quarter Sessions that there were inhabitants who could not keep their children and servants indoors because of the disorderly late night performances. In the early 1800s badger baiting and cock fighting were competitive entertainments. 'Cudgel playing', where 'that man that breaks the most heads and saves his own' could win two guineas with the dexterity of his club and 'single-stick' (as its name suggests a one-handed stick fight), were part of the fun. Ballad singers and puppet shows, peep shows and exhibitions of waxworks, boxing bouts and acrobats entertained the crowds. At night the Square was lit with flaring naphtha lamps. Every September the bells were rung for the Fair and people were allowed, for a small payment, to visit the bell tower, although both were stopped by Canon Codd in 1858. By the early 1900s the fun of the fair had been taken over by steam roundabouts lit by bright electric lights and in later years Townsend's Fair continued the tradition.

Celebrations and Festivities

For centuries the ringing of the church bells marked every significant religious and secular occasion. 'Loyal' and 'thanksgiving' peals were rung to mark royal births, marriages, deaths and coronations, military victories and peace proclamations, as well as the deaths of important national figures. The tolling of the 'minute bell' marked the passing of Beaminster inhabitants. In the later 1600s the churchwardens' accounts recorded payments to the ringers for ringing on Guy Fawkes' Day, St George's Day and Oak Apple Day. The curfew bell marked the start and end of each day. Every morning at 5 o'clock a bell was tolled and it was sounded again at seven o'clock each night. The daily morning bell was rung up to about 1860 and evening bell until about 1870. The ringing out of the old year and ringing in the new was mentioned by Hine in 1914 and is still done today.

National events were celebrated with great enthusiasm and followed a similar pattern of street and house decoration, procession of local organisations and bands, ringing of the church bells and a church service, sports, tea and dancing. Pageantry and spectacle drew large crowds of townsfolk and the procession was a feature in all sorts of celebrations. Club Day was once a most important holiday and, with visiting town bands playing and flying their banners, the club members carried aloft their decorated club sticks processing through the town to the church. After the service the parade continued to Prout Bridge after

George V's silver jubilee, 1935. The parade in East Street.

Beaminster celebrates George V's silver jubilee in the Square, 1935.

which dinner was served at different inns in the town.

The opening of the Horn Hill Tunnel in 1832 was marked by a grand procession and when Princess Victoria (later to be Queen) and her mother the Duchess of Kent came through Beaminster on 30 July 1833 her passage through the tunnel was marked with the firing of cannon which were positioned on the hill above. Garlands of flowers, one surmounted by a crown, were hung across the streets, and every house along her route was decorated with flowers, and laurel and flags were hung from the windows. The church bells rang, a band played 'God save the King' and mounted troops escorted the royal party as it proceeded towards Bridport accompanied by 'immense cheering from the people'.

When, on 28 June 1838, Queen Victoria was crowned there was a distribution of beer and beef to over 400 poor families in the parish. Once more arches and garlands decorated the streets, the bells rang out and parading schoolchildren with nosegays were led by a band. Tea and cakes were served to all, and even at the workhouse the paupers had beef, plum pudding and ale. Celebrations for her golden jubilee in 1887 saw the Ancient Order of Foresters with Robin Hood, Little John, Will Scarlet, Friar Tuck and their 'merrie men' carrying their flags and emblems, followed by the Independent Order of Oddfellows with Faith, Hope and Charity behind their banner. The Beaminster Brass Band led the townspeople and at the rear the last few members of the Friendly Society carried their club sticks – this was to be their last marching appearance in the town. A church service was followed by more parading through the town. A dinner was served in a marquee in the grounds of the manor house, followed by sports and a tea for about 1,000 women and children. After jubilee hymns and prize-giving there was dancing, the grounds and trees were illuminated and there were fireworks. Later that night beacon fires were lit on the hills above the town.

The marriage of Albert Edward, Prince of Wales, in 1863 saw several barrels of cider placed in the Square for all to help themselves and a big bonfire. Edward VII's coronation in 1902 included a torchlight procession and decorated bicycles. The new Institute and Public Hall, opened in 1903, commemorated this event. George V's coronation in 1911 incorporated a cavalcade of people on horseback, on foot and in cars, dressed as historical and mythological characters.

The Beaminster Brass Band was formed in 1878 by George 'Dad' Swaffield and became known as the Beaminster Prize Band in the 1930s when it won the Wessex Band Association Festival. A new uniform of green whipcord with gold and cherry red was introduced in 1935. They added to the pomp and ceremony of formal occasions such as Thanksgiving Services to mark the end of war and Remembrance Days, as well as to the more light-hearted events such as football matches and fêtes.

Above: *Beaminster Band, 1920.*

Below: *Beaminster Silver Band, 1955.* Left to right, back row: *Ronald Andrews, Victor Dawe, Douglas Hutchings (bandmaster), Sidney Poole;* middle row: *Percy Bugler, Charlie Lewis, Albert Tompkins, Pat Woods (née Andrews), Bert Bullock, Maureen Dawe, Peter Riglar, Tony Greenham, Bill House;* front row: *Eric Hayward, Reggie Riglar, Max Lewis, David Bullock, Ronald Hussey.*

Teams, Groups and Societies

Making one's own entertainment was the norm and the town had organisations, clubs and activities to suit every inclination. By about 1845 cricket was played on a field called Long Ground at Hollymoor and continued until about 1866. By 1869 a proper pitch was laid in a field off Tunnel Road and a regular club had been formed. A poem to mark winning the Minor Cup in the 1924–25 season includes the verse:

We got it! Our joy was completed,
We threw up our bats in the air,
Our rivals were now well defeated,
In a game we can wager was fair.

It further relates that the team celebrated rather well and the author, suffering an aching head, vows to keep off the 'Lush' until the cup is won again!

Hunting was a popular pastime and spectators from all walks of life enjoyed the West Dorset and Beaminster Races on Beaminster Down from September 1867 to 1870, as well as horse races which took place regularly in the early 1900s.

Beaminster had a Rugby Union Football Club in

Left: *Bridport and District Cricket Club v MCC in 1898.* Left to right, back row: *F.J. Hutchins (Hon. Sec.), Phillips, G.T. Metcalfe, E.W. Hirst, Tyler, Captain Kindersley, J.N. Williams, Woodcock, W.H. Price, J. Vesey, Moss (umpire);* middle row: *Revd W.V. Jephson, Dr Kitson, Revd C.E. Kindersley, Revd H.R.W. Farrer (Captain of Bridport), H.H. Palairet (Captain MCC), L.C.H. Palairet, R.C.N. Palairet, F.C. Bond, Revd P.T.P. Knott;* front row: *A. Zeally, R. Dewdney, J. Zealley, Carlin, Watts. Revd W.J. Jephson played for Beaminster as opening batsman and opening bowler. Revd P.T.P. Knott played for Broadwindsor and Beaminster as opening batsman. Dr Kitson and R. Dewdney were also bowlers for Beaminster.*

Left: *Beaminster Cricket Club, 1st XI, 1984.* Left to right, back row: *R.A. Walters, D. Baker, K. Grinton, A. Holding, S. Smith, P. Radcliffe, R. Davies, L. Blackburn;* front row: *R.M. Hannam, R. Hansford, R. Bailey, T. Foot, G. Crew, G. Purcell, B.F.M. Page.*

Right: *Beaminster Football Club, West Dorset Cup winners 1924/25.* Left to right, back row: *Arthur Travers, Cecil Poole, Reg Park, Bob Mason;* middle row: *Hubert Hawker, Ernie Cleal, Percy Travers;* front row: *Edgar Frampton, Nigel Stone, Jack Cleal, Albert Bugler, Reg Dawe.*

Left: *Beaminster Football Club. Winners of the West Dorset League and Edwards Charity Cup 1932/33.* Standing: *R. Mason, H. Neller, A.E. Cox, F. Watts, E.G. Turner, R. Neller, R.M. Bugler, W.A Stiby (Hon. Sec.), E Cleal;* left to right, middle row: *H.G. Hawker, G.C. Hunt, V. Rogers;* front row: *C. Tolman, F. Tolman, J. Cleal, F.J. Lumbard.*

Right: *Beaminster Football Team II, winners of the West Dorset Cup, 1948/49.* Left to right, back row: *Michael Bailey, Ron Colborne, Ralph Bugler, Arthur Lambert, Bob Andrews;* middle row: *Gordon Channing, Len Marsh, Jack Cleal, Michael Dart, Donald Bowditch;* front row: *David Bullock, Ron Mansell, Vic Turner, Frank Dawe, Ron Bugler.*

the 1890s but it was discontinued and an Association Football Club replaced it in 1894. By 1912 this team was top of the West Dorset League; in 1920 they finished as runners-up in the Perry Street and District League and further successes followed. Matches were played on pitches in a variety of locations in and around the town, finally settling on what is now the Memorial Playing Fields. Both youth teams and, from the 1950s, senior teams have earned their share of honours.

The Beaminster Rifle Club used the Drill Hall as an indoor rifle range and in the 1932–33 season won the Dorset Miniature Rifle League. One of their most successful members was J.W.R. 'Jack' Newman who won many national honours.

In the 1920s tennis parties were popular with the better-off families. A hockey club started in about 1929 which, although it did not flourish at that time, was the forerunner of the Beaminster Ladies Hockey Club which was formed in 1972.

Music was also important in the town. In 1858 Beaminster had its Musical Society and held concerts with an orchestra and singers all from the town. Local choirs performed in the Public Hall where amateur dramatic productions and lecture programmes offered further opportunities for entertainment.

In 1858 there was a Cottage Garden Society and an annual exhibition of fruits, vegetables and flowers until 1877. In 1896 it was revived as the Beaminster Vegetable and Flower Society, which continued until the 1930s. The Beaminster & District Garden & Allotment Society won a gold medal at RHS Chelsea in 1980 for its Dorset Country Garden. The Beaminster Horticultural Society achieved a notable success in 1998 when a display of cut flowers in the form of a patio garden won first prize at the National Amateur Gardening Show.

From the nineteenth century fraternal organisations were popular amongst the middle and professional classes. The Beaminster Friendship Lodge of the Oddfellows Society was formed in 1858 and met firstly at the New Inn and later at the Congregational church and finally at the Methodist church. Freemasonry was introduced to the town when the Beaminster Manor Lodge was founded in 1872 and met at the White Hart Hotel. The Duke of York Lodge No. 4848 of the Royal Antediluvian Order of Buffaloes was founded in 1923 and met firstly at the New Inn, but later they used the ballroom at the White Hart Hotel, then moved to the Eight Bells, returning to the White Hart in 1945 and were at the Red Lion Hotel from 1964. The Ancient Order of Foresters were also represented in Beaminster.

Beaminster Women's Institute held its first general meeting in 1918 and was, at that time, the only organisation for women in the town. Their fête at Parnham in 1921 offered the delights of a baby show, a variety show, pony rides and tours of the house. In 1922 a 'Fancy Fair' at the manor house featured stalls, boating on the lake and a concert in the house. Some 600 people attended, even in such poor weather!

In 1978 Beaminster twinned with St James in France, forging links which are still strong today. Many other groups, too many to mention here, have made their mark in Beaminster through the years and today the town can boast over 60 clubs and societies. The annual Beaminster Festival sees the town en fête for a week of celebration of the arts when it plays host to local and national performers and artists.

Home-grown entertainment with well-known local people performing in the town. The poster was printed by Hallett, a Beaminster printer.

Signing of the Twinning Charter between Beaminster and St James, September 1978. Left to right: Rick Wood (Secretary), Norman Welsford (President), David Jones (Chairman), Louis Rabel (President), Monsieur Houssard (Mayor of St James), Monsieur Loisyn (Secretary).

Beaminster St Mary's Church Sunday School at Salisbury in 1969. Left to right, back row: Julie Newberry, Linda Trocian, Elaine Barrett, Hugh Barrett; front row: Julia Beechy, Kathleen Lawrence, Jill Down.

Fancy dress for a Red Cross Working Party, probably during the First World War.

Dressing up was clearly something to capture for the family album. These young women seem to be wearing different national costumes. c.1910.

Beaminster Church Choir, 1950. Left to right, back row: Gordon Halson, Giles Frampton, Donald Ireland, Gordon Channing, Irwin Gunning, ? McCulloch, Ted Pannell, Maurice Greenwood (slightly forward): fourth row: ? Pomeroy (cross bearer), George House, ? Barratt, ?, Revd Wheeler, Frank Brooks, Tony Greenham, Neville Hibbs, ?; third row: Geoffrey Mason, Brian Ireland, Ian Moss, ?, ? Tookey, ?; second row: ?, Timothy Fuller, Barry Gibbs, ?, Bruce Tatylor, ? Greenwood, Freddie House; front row, sitting: ?, ?.

Part of the 1st Beaminster Boy Scouts, c.1922. Left to right, back row: George Aitcheson, George? Golby, Jos Barrett, Fred Strevens, Gordon Creed, Cecil Keates, Pat Hann (Assistant Scout Master), Dick Gale, Alf Tatchell, Herbert Keates?; middle row, kneeling: Doug Perkins, Frank Hodder, Dick Read, Fred Tolman, S. Hayward ?; front row, sitting: George Hirst, William 'Bay' Andrews, Les Perkins, Derek Poole, Charles Tolman, Arthur Legg ?.

The dig at Picket Farm, July 2004. The cameraman is filming Time Team's *archaeologists Phil Harding (in hat) and Mick Aston.*

The 'witch' being set upon on her way to market.

South Perrott and Chedington: Parrett and Axe

South Perrott and Chedington (or Cheddington) are neighbouring parishes in the westernmost part of Dorset. Chedington is a street village high on the ridge. The parish is a watershed, the source of the River Axe, which eventually flows into the English Channel, and also the source of the River Parrett which flows through the village of South Perrott in the valley and on to the Bristol Channel. It is this river which gives the village its name, but the origin of it is uncertain. Chedington derives from the Saxon name *Cead* or *Cedda* and simply means 'the village of Cedda's people'. In both cases there were settlements here reaching back to Saxon times, but recent work by Channel 4's *Time Team* near Picket Farm at South Perrott may have revealed something much earlier. Their finds suggest a Neolithic burial site which continued in use during the Bronze Age and was venerated by people of the Roman period who made offerings there. South Perrott is mentioned in the Domesday Survey of 1086 as belonging to Earl Hugh of Abricius. It was formerly held by Alnoth, who apparently bought it together with Catsley at Corscombe from Bishop Alfwolf.

The site of the old manor house in South Perrott is in a field behind the church, where a series of earthworks may still be seen. Originally it belonged to the Mohun family. However, the property was let for generations to the Gibbs (Gibbes) family who were living there in the middle of the seventeenth century when King Charles I stayed there for one night on his march to the west. This is mentioned in a contemporary diary:

Monday 14 October 1644. The King left Chard and kept to the road, dyned at Lord Paulet's and went that night to South Perrott, the first parish in Dorsetshire, leaving Crewkerne two miles short of it, a little on the left hand. The King lay that night at Mr Gibbs, his house, the manor of South Perrott. The troops that night six myles off at Overshot [Evershot]. There coates [coats of arms] are old, in the hall window, where the King lay at Mr Gibbs.

Witchcraft

In 1605 a case was brought to the court of the Star Chamber by Thomas Guppie and his wife, Joan, of South Perrott. Joan was the local wise woman who was reputed to have the power to cure sick humans and animals. Her help was sought by Judith Gibbes, the youngest daughter of William Gibbes, head of the influential local family. Judith had been suffering for some time from internal pains and swellings, and though many doctors had been consulted, they had failed to find a cure. Joan refused to help, possibly realising that her simple remedies would be of no use. However, this refusal was apparently taken as an admission of guilt, in that she had caused Judith's illness in the first place by 'overlooking' her.

It was believed at the time that if you drew blood from a witch she would be deprived of her evil powers, and the Gibbes family made plans accordingly. Three of them, including Judith, approached Joan Guppie as she was riding to market. The following incident, which gave rise to the court case, is recorded as two widely different versions.

The Gibbes family denied any violence. They claimed to have asked Joan politely to dismount and then gently to have lifted her down. They admitted to pricking her with a bramble – but only a little one – which gave rise to two or three drops of blood on her cheek. Judith's sister elaborates on this story, but it is her deposition which accused Joan of witchcraft in some detail. This could have proved very damaging, as an accusation of black magic at this time could lead to death or imprisonment. She claimed that after the 'blooding' Judith's health had improved and that the illness had passed to Joan. This was soon reversed, however, as Joan Guppie recovered and Judith had a relapse and died the following year.

The Guppies on the other hand claimed that Joan was set upon and attacked with pins and brambles by the Gibbes family (who were also armed with staves, daggers and swords) and then dragged from her horse. Fearing for her life she escaped to a nearby house, followed by her attackers who promised further violence.

We may never know the truth, or even the outcome of the case, for it is not recorded. Suffice to say that many parishioners sympathised with Joan. They signed a certificate in 1606 which stated 'Joan Guppie had never done any harm by witchcraft, but contrariwise, has done good to many people.'

Chedington Court and Church

The old manor house at Chedington was replaced by Chedington Court which was built in 1840 for W.T. Hody. In 1893 it became the property of Sir

The reading-room, now Chedington Village Hall.

Chedington church, c.1920.

Chedington rectory, c.1920.

Henry and Lady Peto who kept a 'benevolent and squirearchical eye' over the village until Sir Henry's death in 1947. Sir Henry and Lady Peto were held in considerable respect and regard by the inhabitants as they took great interest in village affairs and often visited the village school. They were well known for their generosity; two examples are the reading-room, which he had built to commemorate Queen Victoria's diamond jubilee, and the restoration of the church.

The original church at Chedington, about which little is known, was built in the grounds of what is now Chedington Court. Remains of tombs can still

be seen there. It was intended that the new church should be built on the same site as before, but when extending the foundations a lot of water from the springs was found, so the site was moved a short distance away. The new church was consecrated in September 1841. The builder, Ellis Daw, lived in South Perrott. He was paid £550 for all the work done to the old church and for building the new church. The church was later restored in 1898 by Sir Henry Peto when a new organ chamber, baptistery and south porch were erected. Sadly it was made redundant in 1981 and is now a private house.

The Church of St Mary in South Perrott stands on the south side of the village. The crossing, transept and nave were built in the thirteenth century and a west porch added later. In the fifteenth century the tower was rebuilt above the crossing and probably heightened, as were the transepts. Early in the sixteenth century a south chapel was added. The chancel and south chapel were rebuilt from 1907–13 and the southeast buttress of the tower was added, owing to subsidence. A fund was started in 1913 to have the three bells in the belfry,

Interior of South Perrott church.

which were considered unsafe, recast and made into six bells. This was done and, together with a new bell frame and cage and the rehanging of the six bells, cost over £360. The new bells were dedicated in 1927. The copper cockerel weather vane was used for years as a shooting target! It was restored and its tail replaced in 1947 by the village blacksmith, Elias Daw.

The Gypsy's Alibi

South Perrott featured briefly in the headlines when it provided witnesses for the celebrated 'Gypsy Alibi' case which had the whole of London agog in 1753. The case centred on a servant girl called Elizabeth Canning who disappeared on New Year's Day and did not return home until 29 January in a dishevelled and exhausted condition. She claimed to have been kidnapped and imprisoned in a house near Enfield, kept by one Mother Wells, and also inhabited by gypsies. One, called Mary Squires was said to be especially 'old and ugly, tall and dark, with a stoop and an underlip of prodigious size'. She and Mother Wells were accused of carrying out an abduction for prostitution as brothel matrons.

Mary Squires' defence was that at the time of the assault she was travelling across Dorset with her son, George, and daughter, Lucy. At first her alibi

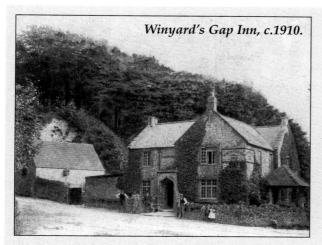

Winyard's Gap Inn, c.1910.

South Perrott girls and a boy in a very large hat!

was not believed. She was found guilty and sentenced to death, the jury being influenced by the magistrate Henry Fielding (no other than the author of *Tom Jones*). Pamphlets and essays were written for both sides and the case became the talk of the town. Many were not happy with the verdict, and after further evidence had come to light, Canning herself was tried for perjury, convicted and transported. The so-called Dorset alibi was now believed and Squires was given a free pardon.

But what was the alibi? It began in South Perrott on 29 December 1751 when Squires and her children were seen in the Red Lion which was near Hill Farm (now Marden Cottage and Three Farthings). They stayed the night here. Next morning, 30 December, they left and were seen at the Three Horseshoes at Wynyards Gap – one source suggests it was the Three Horseshoes on Beaminster Down – where they took breakfast. They were said to have set off from here at about 10a.m. and reached Litton Cheney at 2p.m. This was fast walking over rough terrain, especially for an old woman, who was said by the witness at Wynyards Gap to be 'very unhealthy seemingly, coming up against the hill'. They stayed the night at Litton Cheney, moving on to Abbotsbury, where they stayed until 19 January. Many witnesses were called to verify Mary Squires' statements, but it has been suggested that the gypsies may well have been part of a vast smuggling network which existed in Dorset at the time and that the 'evidence' was worthless. Who knows? Either way, it must have been a great talking point in South Perrott for some time!

Schooling in South Perrott and Chedington

South Perrott's school was built in 1875. It was a single schoolroom, and it appears from the plans that the girls and boys had separate playgrounds, each with separate toilets at the end. The elementary school was built at Chedington in 1850 and included accommodation for a teacher. It was

enlarged in 1900 to cater for 50 children.

The school log-books reveal that Miss Isabella Furmago was the teacher at Chedington from 1877–81 and achieved a very good standard. It was also noted that in 1939 three evacuees from West Ham attended the school. By 1944 pupil numbers had decreased so much that it was decided that both schools should close and the children should attend school at Mosterton. This possibility had clearly been raised for South Perrott some years previously, as a public meeting was held in May 1935 to object most strongly to the proposed closure. On this occasion they must have been successful in their petition as the school stayed open for nearly ten more years.

Trades and Businesses

There were many trades in South Perrott. In 1887 a baker's business was set up by John Oxenbury and it continued trading until 1923. This was in the house known as Hunters Hatch. Another bakery must have existed as there are baking ovens at the Baker's Arms, once one of the four public houses in South Perrott. Of these, only the Coach & Horses remains. There were also boot-makers, cobblers, weavers and candle-makers. There was a laundry at Laurel Cottage, run by Fanny Steer and later by her daughter. Washing was collected in wicker baskets by pony and trap. This business continued until 1940.

For two centuries the Daw family carried on the trades of builder, carpenter, wheelwright and

The Baker's Arms and shop at South Perrott.

The Daws were wheelwrights at South Perrott. In the carpenter's yard, left to right: Phyllis Daw, Isabel Daw (baby), Emma Daw holding hands with Betty Daw, Charles Daw, Elias James Daw, ? Rodford, William Daw, ?, ?, ?, ?. In the front is Elias Guy Daw, aged about five years. c.1915.

Left to right: Elias James Daw and William Daw (blacksmiths), Elias Guy Daw and Charles Daw (wheelwrights). c.1920s.

The yard at Hill Farm, South Perrott. Matt Bartlett is on the right. c.1936.

Blacksmiths Elias James Daw (left) and William Daw, c.1930s.

Chedington village street, c.1920.

South Perrott street scene, c.1900.

undertaker. Ellis Daw who died in 1847 built the churches at Chedington and Mosterton. The last member of the family to run the business, Elias Guy Daw, retired in 1972.

Wartime Legacy

Life changed for many during the Second World War. Evacuees arrived and St James' Secretarial College was moved from London to Chedington Court after the death of Sir Henry Peto. South Perrott was bombed on three occasions, causing some damage. This was probably by German bombers returning from raids and jettisoning their bombs before flying back to base. The local Invasion Committee, who had headquarters at the rectory, decided in 1941 to store emergency rations there and to have an emergency store of tools at Daw's yard. In 1943 it was disclosed that the original team in charge of the fire pump had been reduced to two, the others having been drafted into the Home Guard. Attempts were made to enrol three replacements.

There is a memorial on the hilltop above Wynyards Gap dedicated to the war dead of the 43rd (Wessex) Division of the Territorial Army's campaign from Normandy to the Baltic in 1944–45. Some 16 acres of woodland on either side of the memorial were given to the National Trust in 1949.

The Strode family, c.1900.

Left: *The plaque in Beaminster Museum commemorating James Daniel.*

SACRED TO THE MEMORY OF
JAMES DANIEL, GENT.
AN ANCIENT INHABITANT OF THIS TOWN, AND LONG DISTINGUISHED FOR HIS
CHRISTIAN CHARACTER — HIS PROTESTANT NONCONFORMITY—AND HIS
ZEALOUS DEVOTION TO THE CAUSE OF CIVIL AND RELIGIOUS FREEDOM.
UNDER THE TYRANNY OF KING JAMES THE SECOND,
HE ENDURED MUCH DISQUIETUDE FOR CONSCIENCE SAKE, AND ON ONE OCCASION
NARROWLY ESCAPED FALLING INTO THE HANDS OF THE GOVERNMENT
EMISSARIES WHO WERE APPOINTED TO APPREHEND HIM.
THE BURIAL GROUND, ON THE FAMILY ESTATE IN THIS NEIGHBOURHOOD,
AND IN WHICH HIS REMAINS, AND THOSE OF HIS DESCENDANTS ARE INTERRED,
WAS DESIGNED BY HIM TO INDICATE THE PLACE,
AND COMMEMORATE THE EVENT, OF HIS WONDERFUL CONCEALMENT.
HE DIED IN THE YEAR OF OUR LORD, 1711,
AGED ONE HUNDRED YEARS.
HIS SURVIVING RELATIVES,
OF THE FOURTH, FIFTH, SIXTH, AND SEVENTH GENERATIONS,
HAVE UNITED TO REAR THIS TABLET,
IN HONOUR OF THE PIETY AND PRINCIPLES
OF THEIR PATRIARCHAL ANCESTOR.
1835.
TEMPORA MUTANTUR.

Below: *Beaminster Volunteers at Burton Bradstock Camp, 1869.* Left to right, standing includes: *(Fag) Tom Gibbs, (Privates) A.V. Pine, C. Hann, W. Bugler, E. Toleman, Sergeant J. Hine, T. Meech, J. Keech, J. Long, S. Cox, T. Bugler (a Bridport volunteer), W.T. Bugler (Broadwindsor), (boy) Udall;* front row: *(boy) S. Hann, Corporal W.J. Jefford, (Private) A. Meech, (Bugler) Hughes (Bridport), (Privates) T. Guy, W. Beament.*

Left: *This 1860 daguerreotype shows Thomas Cox of Beaminster (1799–1860), who was one of the soldiers who guarded Napoleon in exile on St Helena between 1815 and 1817. After his discharge he returned to his home in East Street.*

Right: *Edward Collard Smith in the uniform of the Dorset Yeomanry, c.1900.*

Chapter 11

For King and Country

In times of war the men and women of this corner of West Dorset have played their part. Fear of invasion by sea put maritime Dorset among the forefront of the realm's defences. Even before the Armada scare of 1588, when Philip of Spain sent his fleet to invade England, surveys were made to confirm the preparedness of the kingdom. Dorset was divided into eight sub-divisions of which the Beaminster area was one. Maps were annotated with information about the availability of men, carts and horses, mills and ovens and their capacity for bread production, livestock numbers and quantities of grain, flour and potatoes held in store. Muster rolls listed the number of men between the ages of 16 and 30 along with details of their arms equipment. In 1542 there were 131 men named for Beaminster and Langdon.

From 1642 the English Civil War threw the country into turmoil as battles raged the length and breadth of the land. In 1644 soldiers of the Royalist army of Prince Maurice were occupying Beaminster which was generally Parliamentarian in sympathy. Their stay is remembered for the fire which engulfed a large part of the town (see Chapter 3).

A Miraculous Escape

In 1685 there was an attempt to overthrow the Catholic James II and replace him with the Protestant James, Duke of Monmouth, illegitimate son of Charles II. The story is told of one of the Duke's followers, a Beaminster attorney, James Daniel, who fought at the Battle of Sedgemoor. He was an important figure in the town and a reward was offered for his capture. He went to nearby Knowle and hid in a barn, concealing himself beneath some straw which covered the floor. Almost as soon as he was hidden his pursuers, who had searched his premises and been informed of his probable destination, arrived and swords were thrust into the straw. Amazingly he was not discovered. In gratitude for his miraculous escape he decided that he should be buried there. The site, since called Daniel's Knowle, became the family's private burial-ground. A marble memorial in the former Congregational chapel, now Beaminster Museum, records that he died aged 100 years.

Other Beaminster men were involved in the rebellion and 19 faced the infamous Judge Jeffreys at the Bloody Assizes in Dorchester in September 1685, charged with being 'Wanting from their Homes in the tyme of the Rebellion'. The punishment if convicted was hanging or transportation. Four were convicted of high treason and deported; others may have been executed or possibly discharged.

Napoleon and Beaminster

At the time of the 'Great Terror' (1796–1805), when Napoleon threatened the invasion of England, 84 townsmen of Beaminster formed themselves into an infantry corps called the Beaminster Loyal Town Volunteers. It was founded in June 1798 and commanded by Samuel Cox jnr. In his *History of Beaminster* Richard Hine tells of a night in 1799 when an Assembly was sounded:

... which so alarmed the people that nearly all the men, and women too, gathered in the Fore-place to bid farewell to the gallant Volunteers, many of whom they feared never to see again. A special messenger had to be sent to North Field house for the Ensign (Joseph Bishop), who having been recently married had a most affecting farewell with his wife, whom the messenger had almost forcibly to part, to get the band complete. A private named Bartlett, who lived in St Mary Well Street, was at first too frightened to answer the summons. Eventually they all assembled and were thanked by the Captain for their bravery and discipline.

Tradition says that the Volunteers marched towards Bridport but before they got there a message reached them that it was a false alarm.

The Battle of Trafalgar in 1805 saw local men in action. Robert Bowsey of Beaminster, aged 27, served on the *Temeraire* – the ship later immortalised in Turner's painting. On *Belleisle* another Beaminster man John Harrison, aged 29, was a career sailor who had enlisted in 1799. He was eventually discharged in 1815 and awarded the Naval General Service Medal with Trafalgar Clasp. Two Broadwindsor men were involved in the famous battle: John Bradford, aged 23, was aboard Nelson's flagship *Victory* and William Squires, aged 25, was a crew member on *Naiad*. John Dunn of Stoke Abbott had been a labourer when he enlisted in 1801; he served on *Spartiate* and left the navy in 1815. William Sandeford of Netherbury on *Defiance* was, at 43, the oldest of the local sailors serving at Trafalgar.

Thomas Cox (1777–1860) of East Street fought in the Peninsular Wars. He joined the army in 1799 and was wounded at the Battle of Salamanca in 1812. In 1815 he sailed on *Bucephalus* to guard Napoleon in exile on St Helena. He was one of only 16 men

Some of the 51 Boer War officers who came to convalesce at Hooke Court, 1899-1902. Most had suffered from dysentery and enteric fever, and had injuries which varied in severity. English, Scottish, South African and Australian officers are shown here.

Lieut Herbert Hugh Cowie, Bechuanaland Rifles.

Lieut Alexander Livingstone Bruce, 16th Queen's Lancers.

Captain Robert Gordon, DSO, Queensland Light Infantry.

Lieut Arthur J. Peebles, Suffolk Regiment.

Lieut Hugh Alfred Cholmley, 7th Dragoon Guards.

Above: *Lieut W.W. Simmons Lynn, 4th Royal Lancashire Regiment (Militia).*

Left: *Lieut Frank H. Charlton, Kings Dragoon Guards.*

Right: *Surgeon Oswald Challis, Royal Army Medical Corps.*

awarded the Sergeant's Regimental Medal for Salamanca. Legend has it that the award was at the instigation of Napoleon himself who could not believe that his guards from the 53rd Regiment of Foot had not been 'marked' for their service. There is only one of these medals known to be in existence today – and it belonged to Thomas Cox.

The Beaminster Volunteers were disbanded in 1844 but were reformed in 1859 when the country was again threatened with invasion. A total of 26 men from Beaminster, Netherbury and Mosterton also formed a sub-division of the 1st Dorset Rifles Volunteers. In 1875 a Detachment of the 1st DRV was formed at Netherbury.

Other Major Conflicts

At the end of the nineteenth century British forces were again in action, this time in South Africa against the Boers. Beaminster had the honour of sending to the front line, second only to Dorchester, the largest number of volunteers from Dorset. The Company of Volunteers from Dorset was commanded by Captain Kitson of Beaminster. They embarked on 3 April 1900 for South Africa. One Beaminster soldier, George Swaffield, kept a small notebook in which he recorded his experiences on his journey to the front and his first engagements:

... we got on the hill & stopped the night intrenching ourselves we could hear firing. We had an awful night

THE WAR
LORD KITCHENER
HAS ASKED FOR
100,000
RECRUITS
TO SERVE THEIR
KING & COUNTRY
IN
THE ARMY
NEAREST RECRUITING OFFICE,
S.-S.-Major Froome,
Institute, Beaminster.

Recruiting for the First World War. Lord Kitchener made a special appeal to rural workers to join up once the harvest was over.

Dorset Yeomanry, c.1915. Seated centre is Lieut Col Troyte-Bullock and to his left is Major J.B.H. Godden. They mustered at Sherborne where this photograph may have been taken, prior to embarkation at Avonmouth, first seeing action at Gallipoli and later, in 1916, at Agagir in Egypt.

what with fire and wind we had to fight against the Grass fire but it was no use we had to carry our things through the flames on to the burnt grass the next morning we had to make some more trenches to protect ourselves & before long we were under fire we had a lot of Boer snipers all round us & as soon as we show ourselves had a shower of bullets it was our first experience under fire we lost two of our chaps in making the trenches... we had to spend another night on that hill the wind and rain was awful & the dust was blinding we had a relief next day & saw the Artillery shelling the hills around Laing's nek...

On their return in June 1901 the streets of Beaminster were decorated and the townspeople gave the soldiers a hero's welcome with a torchlight procession and a welcome address from the Chairman of the Parish Council. All received the Freedom of the Boroughs of Bridport and Dorchester and each was awarded a marble clock bearing the inscription:

Presented to...
by the Inhabitants of Beaminster,
on his return home after serving his country
as a member of the Volunteer Service Corps
in South Africa
1900–1901

The year 1914 saw the outbreak of the First World War in which 36 Beaminster men lost their lives. Their names, together with the names of those who served, can be seen on plaques taken from the memorial in the Square which are now fixed to the churchyard wall of St Mary's.

William Rhodes-Moorhouse VC

William Rhodes-Moorhouse (1887–1915) of Parnham was the first airman to be awarded the Victoria Cross. As a young man he was fascinated by speed; first motorbikes and then racing cars were his passion. In 1911 he designed, manufactured and flew his own aeroplane under San Francisco's Golden Gate Bridge winning himself the Harbour Prize of £1,000. He is recorded as the first man to fly across the English Channel with two passengers.

When war broke out in 1914 he joined the Royal Flying Corps. In April 1915 he was ordered to blow up a railway junction. His solo mission was a success but his biplane came under a barrage of enemy fire. Wounded but unwilling to land behind enemy lines

In 1915 William Rhodes-Moorhouse of the Royal Flying Corps became the first airman to be awarded the Victoria Cross, the highest military award given only for the most conspicuous bravery or act of valour.

The gun, before being mounted on its plinth in the Square. Its inscription reads:

This 77 Field Gun was captured by the British from the Germans in the Great European War 1914–1918. It was presented to the town of Beaminster by His Majesty's War Office in 1919 in recognition of the very gallant deed of Lieutenant Rhodes-Moorhouse, Parnham, Beaminster, for which he was awarded the VC. He being the first member of the RFC to win this most Coveted Distinction.

The unveiling ceremony of the war memorial and gun commemorating William Rhodes-Moorhouse VC by Air Marshal Sir Hugh Trenchard on 2 January 1921. Plaques were mounted around the plinth recording the names of all the Beaminster men who served in the First World War. The gun was removed in 1940 and sold for salvage because it was feared that its presence might draw enemy fire.

and risk the capture of his plane he continued towards his base at Merville but received another serious injury as he flew only 100 feet back across the German lines. Terribly wounded he completed the return flight, made a perfect landing and made his report. He died 24 hours later and was posthumously awarded the Victoria Cross. His body was returned to his parents' home at Parnham House, where his coffin lay for one night in the great hall before he was buried 'on the top of the hill' above Parnham where he had planned to build a little house for himself, his wife and his son.

The Second World War

After only two decades of peace war came again.

Beaminster Wartime Fire Service. Left to right, back row: *Bill Emery, Bill Barter, Cecil Bevis, Arthur Travers, Vic Turner, Alfred Pomeroy, Fred Collin, Charlie Park, Fred Tolman;* front row: *George Legg, Trevor Rendell, Jack Newman, Francis Bugler, ? Gibbs, John Newman?, Fred Forsey.*

Beaminster & Broadwindsor Sections of the Dorset Special Constabulary. Left to right, back row: *(Special Constables) A. Morris, J. Sprackling, F. Moon, C. Willey, J. Poole, W.C. Poole, J. Strawbridge, R.E. Bartlett, L. Pitcher, F. Saunders;* middle row: *(Special Constables) T. Meech, F.H. Studley, E Poole, A.J. Dart, F. Bridle, R. Ashford, W. Thomas, G. Waldren, R. Marks, B. Mapstone, A.G. Neal;* front row:

(Special Constables and other ranks as shown) J. Eveleigh, D. Wyatt, F. Andress, E. Cleal (Sergeant), L. Skyrm (Ex-Sergeant), E.D. Cox (Inspector), J.J. Bartlett (Sergeant), F. Poole (Sergeant), R. Ryall, S. Chaffey.

Above: *Beaminster Home Guard, c.1941.* Left to right, back row: *R. Colborne, K. Cleal, H. Pomeroy, ?, W. Sykes, S. Matterface, A. Pomeroy, F. Dawe, H. Bacon, C. Tomlinson;* middle row: *A. Gibbs, B. Gale, W. Watts, H. Hawker, Watts, G. House, V. Dawe, V. Kingham, Graveson, J. Gardner, J. Vickery, ?, J. Symonds, Rundle, Hussey, ?, A. Mounter, G. Hunt;* front row: *Cpl Brooks, Cpl Stone, Sgt W. Baker, Sgt C. Dawe, Capt. Chadwick, Maj. Hornor, Lieut Colborne, W/O W. Bugler, Sgt G. House, Sgt B. Tizzard, Cpl Mann, Cpl W. Nightingale..*

Right: *Cpl Charles Smith of Manor Farm Stoke Abbott, No. 1 Mounted Platoon, 'E' Company Home Guard, 1942. The platoon of ten patrolled the open countryside, keeping watch for German parachutists.*

Demonstration of wartime fire fighting and rescue by the Fire Brigade and Auxiliary Fire Service for War Weapons Week, 1941.

Sunday 3 September 1939 was a fine morning with people going about their normal activities when the Prime Minister, Neville Chamberlain, made his radio broadcast telling the nation that the country was at war with Germany. Men were conscripted to the forces or joined up voluntarily and the authorities were prepared for war on the Home Front. Gas masks and sandbags were issued, materials were purchased to repair war-damaged houses, arrangements were made to deal with civilian deaths caused by gas or air raids, and in the town, a site for a mortuary was identified. J.W. Sill, the local pharmacist, was appointed Gas Identification Officer.

By the autumn of 1939 ARP posts had been set up in Beaminster and the surrounding villages, wardens recruited and equipped. Food and Fuel Offices were opened in Fore Place to deal with the administration of rationing. The fire brigade, based in a courtyard behind the Town Offices and later supplemented by an auxiliary fire service unit, prepared for incendiary devices and high explosive bombs.

A blackout was imposed from 1 September 1939. Fortunately Beaminster folk were used to the dark as the only streetlights were in the central part of the town. There were those, however, who did not manage to comply with the new regulations and a crop of prosecutions at Beaminster's Petty Sessions were heard with fines imposed on a pedestrian with a bright torch, cyclists with uncovered front lights, car drivers with unobscured headlamps and householders with ineffectively screened windows. The cellars of the White Hart Hotel were offered as a

public air-raid shelter. One resident recorded the air-raid siren on the roof of the police station sounding 360 times between 5 July 1940 and 16 June 1944. Luckily the only 'civilian' casualties were some cows.

By July 1941 the district hosted 734 evacuee children. Schools needed to adapt, one teaching evacuees in the morning and local children in the afternoon, another by relocating classes to an old mill in order to allow the evacuees the use of classrooms. Air-raid drill appeared in the curriculum and pupils helped to dig school trenches. A local child remembered:

> There was a whole school brought down from London – John Perrin School in Acton... My brother and I sat here whilst mother went off. Supposedly she was going to come back with two little girls, that's what she was prepared to look after, but when she came back about ten o'clock at night she came back with four teenage boys.

For children unused to rural life the evacuee experience was very strange. An evacuee recalled, 'On my first night I lay hearing animal night calls so unusual for a town boy.'

'E' Company (Beaminster) Home Guard was based at the Drill Hall on Stoke Road. Nearly half the men were First World War veterans with fighting experience. Major Hornor commanded and Leonard Colborne, the town's postmaster, was sergeant. Shooting practice took place at butts towards Stoke Abbott and grenade practice in sandbagged 'zigzag' trenches on Beaminster Down. The lookout post was above the Horn Hill Tunnel on Seamark Hill. A mounted patrol of up to ten men led by local doctor, Herbert Lake, covered the more sparsely populated areas. At least one local lady, Mrs Kathleen Tennant is known to have ridden with them as they sought to intercept German parachutists.

In 1940 the threat of invasion was very real. Secretly a small group of men had been formed into an innocent-sounding Auxiliary Unit. Local farmer, John Wakely, was recruited to lead a team to carry out sabotage, guerrilla warfare and surprise attacks against the invaders. His men were Stanley Bale, Ernest and George Raymond, Douglas Perkins, who was replaced when called up by Henry Higgins, and Frank Ivory, replaced on call-up by Vic Downton. One of them recalled their instructions should an invasion ever take place:

> The secret Home Guard was so secret even our parents didn't know. When the invasion started we were to creep out at night and bring down the trees to block the tunnel with this explosive that looked like a string of sausages. And then we'd be sent to set fire to all the vehicles, even our parents', so that no-one could use them.

The resistance unit operated from a secret under-

Air Training Corps. Left to right, left wing: *Colin Phillips, Peter Hitchcock, Gordon Channing, Stanley Leach, Giles Frampton, Lambert Everleigh, Arthur Lawrence, Bob Andrews;* on engine: *Cyril Poole;* centre, standing: *Norman Welsford;* right wing: *Arthur Lambert, Brian Peters, John Laramy, 'Jungle' Jennings, Jim House, John Cook, Larry Burns, Tony Stevens.*

ground operational base hidden in woodland on the hills above Beaminster, supplied with enough explosives and ammunition for 14 days. Armed with combat knives and revolvers these men, all farmers or farm workers, knew the local terrain intimately.

The town's ARP controller warned that the memorial gun on a plinth in the Square was so conspicuous from the air that it was certain to draw enemy attack. The gun was removed and sold for salvage.

On 16 February 1943 a damaged German Dornier bomber returning from a raid on Swansea, crashed into South Buckham farmhouse on a ridge above the town killing the crew. By some miracle no-one in the house was injured.

New faces appeared in the town as troops from all parts of the country came and went. In October 1939 the 210th (Sussex) Field Company marched into Beaminster. A Scottish piper played the bagpipes in the Square every day during his regiment's stay. For a time the Royal Medical Corps was billeted at Bridge House and a Light Aid Detachment had a workshop next to Perry & Perry's garage in Broadwindsor Road.

Southern Command requisitioned the Square as a car park for Motor Transport from December 1939. The council was concerned that 'the large influx of troops and others' might be too much for the drains!

Numbered amongst these 'others' were the Land Girls. Gangs of girls were transported by lorry from the Women's Land Army hostel on the outskirts of the town to work on the farms. They hedged and ditched, drove tractors, cared for livestock, harvested grain and flax, dug potatoes and mangolds. Some Land Girls were employed full-time on individual farms, either living on the farm or lodging in the town. Others came to Horn Park Dairy, a separate training establishment, to be taught milking.

As the war progressed young women left to join the women's services and young men continued to be called up. The Women's Institute sent Christmas parcels to 'our boys and girls serving in His Majesty's forces abroad'. The young people of the area also played their part. Boys could join the Air Training Corps or the Army Cadet Force, and the Girls' Training Corps cooked breakfasts for the Home Guard and undertook first-aid training. Boy Scouts collected waste paper in the town and villages and Girl Guides picked foxgloves to be turned into the drug digitalis.

Land Girls (from left) *Eirwen Evans* (seated), *Rosemary Lawford, Marjorie Cheeseman and Mary Andrews outside the Beaminster WLA hostel with the War Agricultural Executive Committee van in which they were driven out to the farms each day.*

Girls Training Corps. This picture includes: *Alma Burt, Christine Studley, Nesta Bugler, Kathleen Cunnings, Peggy Rendall (Stoke Abbott), Muriel House, Mary Poole, Mrs Violet Hurst, Mrs Kathleen Tenant, Audrey Pigeon, Una Parsons, Muriel Corcoran, Monica Dart, Cecily Tomlinson, Mary Hallett.*

Above: 'The Brit' Spitfire. Beaminster and Bridport's Spitfire Fund raised enough money to 'buy' Spitfire R7062.

Left: Reggie Riglar, Jim House, John Page, Peter Page and Richard Wetherden with an American GI on a jeep in Church Street, 1944.

In 1943 American troops arrived. The 16th Infantry Regiment set up their HQ at Parnham House. Quonset huts (similar to the British Nissen hut) appeared in Parnham's parkland and on the other side of the Bridport Road. Cannon Company had its motor pool at the top of Fleet Street, the Anti-Tank Company was billeted at the Red Lion Hotel, the Medical Detachment were above a hairdresser's at Prout Bridge and soldiers were accommodated all over the town. Beaminster was suddenly a livelier place with more dances and bands at the Public Hall, candy and gum for the children, and many 'goodies' which had not been seen for years in the shops. In May 1944 the town fell quiet again; the Americans had left for the D-Day landings on the Normandy beaches.

By the end of the war local people had 'Dug for Victory', knitted 'Comforts for the Troops', helped buy a Spitfire, given up their saucepans and railings, attended demonstrations of wartime cookery and operated a Meat Pie Scheme for rural workers. Servicemen and women began to return home but the town was left to mourn those who had made the ultimate sacrifice for their country. Early in the new millennium the Royal British Legion still leads the town in remembrance every year.

Beaminster area's War Weapons Week in July 1941. Captain Simon Wingfield Digby MP addressed the gathering and the town and villages raised £75,054.10s.11d. to support the war effort.

Right: Remembrance Day, 1999. Laying wreaths at St James, France with representatives of the Beaminster Branch of the British Legion.

Stoke Abbott: Ringed By Hills

Stoke Abbott is another farming village with origins before Domesday. It has had various names such as Stoke (1086), Stook, and Abbot(s) Stoke. Its largest recorded population, 826, was in 1851 but at the time of writing it stands at about 200. Stoke Abbott is a parish of 2,327 acres including Waddon Hill, a Roman base for the advance of the 2nd Legion to Exeter in AD43. At Waddon Hill a Roman sword scabbard and coins were found during quarrying between 1876 and 1878, which are now in the British Museum. Lewesdon Hill is also in the parish and is considered the highest point in Dorset.

In 1939 Stoke Abbott was described by Arthur Mee:

It is an enchanted place, with hanging orchards and bright gardens ringed by hills, its banks alive with primrose and violet and anemone, its cottages aglow with wallflower, the floor of its copses sparkling with the joy of spring.

The village has narrow hollow lanes with ferns and overhanging trees. Most of the houses are situated along the original medieval main route through the village and are built above the flood level. The buildings are mainly seventeenth to nineteenth century origin, built of local stone and include several gentry houses. There are 34 listed buildings. There are terraces of strip lynchets, a medieval farming system, at Chart Knolle.

Church and Worship

There has been a church in the village since Saxon times. The oldest part of the current building dates back to the twelfth century, between AD1100 and AD1150. The remainder has been built at various times in the thirteenth, fourteenth and fifteenth centuries. There was formerly an old building adjoining the churchyard called the Church House, inhabited by the poor of the parish. In 1520 the then Abbot of Sherborne, John Meare, had transferred by lease to the churchwardens of Stoke Abbott a piece of ground, which was once the court place of the manor, on which to erect a new house for the common profit of the parish. It was duly erected but after the dissolution of the abbey in 1539 two farmers of Stoke Abbott, William Gollop and Thomas Googe, set up a claim to the title of the house and removed the parishioners. A Bill was filed in Chancery for redress and after much further litigation the matter was finally settled in 1573 in favour of the tenants of the parish, who, it was ruled, should hold and enjoy the Church House without molestation from the farmers. Justice done!

According to a return of 1650 the rector of the parish received tithes of corn, hay, wool, lamb, cow-white, pigs and apples amounting to £86. He was obliged to keep a bull for the servicing of the parishioners' cows. They had to pay the rector 1d. for every garden, 5d. for every milch cow and 4d. for every milch heifer in lieu of the tithes of milk and calves.

The church was restored in 1876/8 when the gallery was removed. It has a peal of five bells dating from 1470 to 1764. The clock is, like those at Beaminster and Netherbury, without a face and strikes on the hour. According to *Hunt's Directory* of 1867 the church was struck by lightning in 1828 breaking all the windows, bursting open the doors, melting the wires of the chimes and splitting the tower. If this is true then the tower was obviously rebuilt.

William the Conqueror first instituted curfews. Much later, Queen Elizabeth I ordered that from 1583 when the curfew was rung in the evening the public house should close. The curfew bell used to be rung at 5.30a.m. daily to awaken the village. The morning bell is still sounded, although a little later than of old! In the past a small piece of land called the Curfeu Plot, on the west side of the street opposite the rectory, was held by whoever was the clerk of the parish. The donor is unknown.

There was a Congregational church from 1786 when a private house was licensed as a private place of worship. A chapel was opened in 1838 after a subscription was started and the land was given by a Mr Conway from Beaminster.

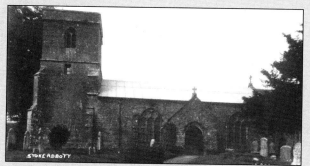

Stoke Abbott church.

Murder Most Foul

Sarah Ann Guppy was murdered here on 30 April 1858. She was described in a handbill, published by Frosts of Bridport, as of diminutive stature, rather deformed, an easy and good-natured woman, quick, intelligent, but never very healthy. She lived in lodgings with her mother in the semi-detached cottage rented by James Seale and belonging to John Hutchings, who lived in the other half of the building. She was seen alive at 2p.m. At about 4p.m. a lot of smoke was seen coming from the cottage by labourers in the fields who ran to find her lying dead on the floor with her throat cut with a four-inch gash. Another James Seale, aged 20, had been seen by Jane Cornick, aged 70, coming from the cottage at about the right time with blood on his hand and on his trousers. At the inquest held the next day by the coroner, S.S. Cory Esq., with a jury of 18 people, James Seale was accused of her murder. He was described as a diminutive young man of 20, although looking three years younger, his head covered with a profusion of hair, an indolent fellow, dishonest, already having spent four months at the treadmill and once privately whipped for stealing 1s.10d. from a child. His was the last recorded public hanging at Dorchester on 10 August 1858.

Stoke Abbott School

In 1859 an elementary school was erected, now the Village Hall, on the instigation of the rector Dr Richards on a site to the north of the church. The school was enlarged in 1879 and in 1906 it was recorded that it held 100 children with an average attendance of 65. The school was finally closed in 1950 since when the children have gone by bus to Beaminster.

Trades and Businesses

Amongst the trades people in the village in 1867 there was a shopkeeper Thomas Conway; a miller and farmer Mrs Mary Bowditch at Brimley Mill; two carpenters William Clare and William Hann jnr; a carpenter and blacksmith Richard Clare; two boot- and shoemakers Robert Elliott and Edward Holland (also the assistant overseer and collector of poor rates); a milliner and dressmaker Mrs Harriett Dommett; two further dressmakers, Mrs Emily Hopkins and Miss Sarah Staple; a baker and grocer Mrs Sarah Gill; and a spinner, flax and tow manufacturer George Macey at Clenham Mill, Netherbury. The Post Office receiver was Edward Holland and the publican of the New Inn, James Harwood, was also a mason.

In 1895 'There used to be a lot of flax grown. Most of the corn was cut by scythes except the wheat which was cut by the old reaper or trapper...'

Lower Farm dates from 1545, Stoke Farm from 1613 and Court Orchard from 1761. According to Hutchins, Chartknolle was anciently part of the manor of Stoke Abbas and Charterhay. In the nineteenth century it was owned by Lieut. Col Samuel Symes Cox for many years before he lived at Beaminster Manor House.

The Workhouse Bridge

The Beaminster Union Workhouse was built at Stoke Water in 1836 and had between 70 and 100 inmates until as recently as 1939 when it was occupied by the army. The stone bridge in the grounds is inscribed, 'This bridge was erected in the year 1795 at the joint expense of the town of Beaminster and the parish of Stoke Abbott. Briscoe the mason.'

The Sick Club

A Sick Club was formed in 1879 by the Revd William Austin-Gourlay out of a Friendly Society that had existed for 10 years. Sick Clubs offered help to the poorer members of the village as they were required to contribute a small amount of money into a fund and those who were ill could draw money out according to their contributions. Club Day was always held on the first Friday in June when the houses and streets were tidied, covered with bunting and streamers and a procession occurred with members carrying flags and staves with ribbons, preceded by the Beaminster Band. The parade was followed by a service in the church and a feast in the afternoon at the school.

Stoke Sick Club, c.1906, with the Street Fair showing stalls selling sweet rock outside the Anchor Inn. The three women with white aprons are, from left to right, *Ada Welch, Mary Canterbury and Eilfred Swaffield.*

Stoke Abbott Today

In 2007 many of the village dwellings are now second homes. Although there is no longer a shop, the public house is still going strong.

Stoke Abbott Sick Club outside the Manor House in 1912.

Right: *Court Orchard, Stoke Abbott, c.1901.*

Below: *Manor Farm, 1936, with a view to the villagers' cottages in the street.*

Right: *Mary Hallett, known as Bendigo, 1906.*

Below: *Charles and Sarah Canterbury, c.1906. They ran a carriers business.*

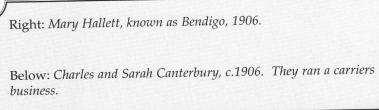

Thatched cottage on the right that belonged to Mr G. Woolmington, c.1906. The cottage burned down in 1907.

Stoke Abbott WI, 1920. Left to right, back row: Daisy Gillingham, Vicki Swaffi(eld?), Lucy Clarke, Blanche Lancashire, Janie Lenshall, ? Puckhams (housekeeper), Irene Meech; front row: Mary Canterbury, Mary Meech, Vivienne Thorne.

Below and right: *Stoke Abbott cottagers and the village street, c.1906.*

Sources

In addition to documents and oral histories accessed from the Beaminster Museum Reference Section, original material and publications in the Dorset History Centre and information offered by individuals the following sources are acknowledged.

Beaminster Area Team, *Team News*
Beaminster Society magazines, *Around and About Beaminster* (various)
Bennett, W., *The Toller Whelme Book* (1987)
Bettey, J.H., *Man and the Land: Farming in Dorset 1846–1996* (1996)
Bettey, J.H., *Rural Life in Wessex* (1977)
Bridport News
Brook, Barbara (compiler), *Salway Ash Memories* (1995)
Country Life Magazine
Cox, Eric H., *Corscombe* (1970)
Dorset: the County Magazine
Dorset Federation of Women's Institutes, Dacombe, Marianne, R. (ed.) *Dorset Upalong Downalong* (undated)
Eedle, M. de G., *A History of Beaminster* (1984)
Eedle, M. de G. & Paul, R.E., *The Death & Times of John Daniel* (1987)
Fägersten, Anton, *Place-Names of Dorset* (1933)
French, G., *Stoke Abbott: West Dorset* (4th edn, 1996)
Harris, Duncan, *Paupers, Dukes and a Prince: Hooke – A West Dorset Village* (2005)
Hine, R., *History of Beaminster* (1914)
Hutchins, *History of Dorset* (3rd edn, 1874)
Large, E.H., *Broadwindsor: A Short History* (undated)
Lemmey, P., *A History of Halstock* (1986)
Malan, A.N., *Solomon Caesar Malan* (1897)
Milne, Taylor, *A History of Broadwindsor, Dorset* (undated)
Mosterton Afternoon WI, *Village History of Mosterton* (1984)
Netherbury Parish Pack (2005)
Nightingale, J.E., *Church Plate of Dorset* (1889)
Parrett and Axe WI (compilers), *A Village History of Chedington and South Perrott* (1983)
Parsons, G.J., *The Parsons Family:* vol 1 (2002)
Pulman, Revd George P.R., *The Book of the Axe* (4th edn, 1875)
Sadler, M. & P. (compilers), *Corscombe Through The Ages* (undated)
Stephens, Florence M., *Florrie: A Mythe Childhood* (2005)
Taylor, Christopher, *Dorset* (1970)
Treves, Sir F., *Highways and Byways of Dorset* (1906)
Usher, Revd R., *A Short History of Netherbury Church and Parish* (reprint 1948)
Woodward, D.R., *A History of Beaminster & Netherbury Grammar School* (2005)

Subscribers

Mrs S. Adams (née Whitmarsh), Yeovil
John and Marjorie Aird, Beaminster, Dorset
Ian and Margot Allman, Hursey, Dorset
Nicholas A. Amor, Bridport, Dorset
Andrew and Carolyn Amos, Winslow, Buckingham
Joyce Ascott (née Brinson), Beaminster
Dr John R. Ashwood, Beaminster, Dorset
Frieda Attwood, Beaminster, Dorset
Alan Baker, Evershot
Hayley Baker, Bradpole, Dorset
Professor and Mrs John Barnard, Beaminster, Dorset
Kath and Jack Barnett, Beaminster, Dorset
Roy and Sandy Barrett, Beaminster, Dorset
Una Barter (née Grain and Fraser), Chandlers Ford, Hants
R.S. and J.D. Bartlett, Broadwindsor, Dorset
T.J. and K.M. Bartlett, South Perrott, Dorset
Douglas and Lynda Beazer, Beaminster, Dorset
Joy Beazer, Beaminster
Mr and Mrs J.N. Beeny, Beaminster, Dorset
Raymond John Beer, Bridport, Dorset
Graham Belsey, Beaminster
Edmund H. Berry, Beaminster, Dorset
Canon Timothy and Mrs Joan Biles
Alexandra Mackay Binnie, Beaminster, Dorset
Aileen Bishop, Broadwindsor, Dorset
Bernard Bonte, Cesson Sevigne, Rennes, France
Rachel A. Bowditch, Beaminster
C.G.C. Bowditch, Chideock, Dorset
Bridport Museum Trust
Doris Britton, Bradford, West Yorks
Christine L. Broad, Beaminster, Dorset
Marjorie and John Broadhead, Beaminster
Jack Brooks, Beaminster, Dorset
Verity J. Brooks, Edinburgh
Mr and Mrs R.J. Brooks, Ammanford, Dyfed
Steve and Sue Brown, High Wycombe, Bucks
Nadine Brummer, Beaminster, Dorset
Carey Buckler, Melplash Court Farm
Robert Buckler, Melplash Court Farm
Nell Buckler, Melplash Court Farm
Elsa Buckler, Melplash Court Farm
Nigel and Gill Budden, Broadwindsor
June Bugler, Beaminster
Ralph Bugler, Beaminster
Tony Bugler, Beaminster, Dorset
William R. Bugler, Bridport, Dorset
Richard G. Bugler, Beaminster
Wm John Bugler 1877-1960, Beaminster
Charlotte Bullock, Tetbury and Beaminster
Mr K. Bullock, Mosterton, Dorset

David Bullock, Beaminster, Dorset
Norma Burford, Bengeo, Hertford
Richard Burleigh, Charmouth, Dorset
Andrew and Fiona Burwood, Beaminster, Dorset
Rolf and Margrit Busenhart, Greifensee, Switzerland
Mr D.J.H. Butler, Hooke Estate
Pat and Ron Cabble, Mosterton, Dorset
Derek Caen, Tunnel Road, Beaminster
Norman and Doreen Calvert, Crewkerne, Somerset
Timothy. M. Chandler, Kingstone, Herefordshire
John A. Chandler, Harrogate, North Yorkshire
Patrick and Ann Chapman, Stoke Abbott, Dorset
Eric Cheeseman, Poole, Dorset
Windsor, Deborah and Lily Chorlton, Beaminster
Rod Church, Beaminster, Dorset
Cyril Clark, Mosterton, Dorset
Sue Clarke, Bickington, Devon
Eddie and Anne Clegg, Lancashire
Elaine Clifft, Beaminster, Dorset
M.M.S. Cooper, Bridport, Dorset
Terence K. Cooper, Beaminster, Dorset
David Cooper, Little Berkhamsted, Hertford
The Copisarow Family, Meerhay
John A. Cowie, Beaminster, Dorset
Mary and Fred Cox of Mosterton
Olive Crabbe, Beaminster
Wendy Cranswick, Beaminster, Dorset
Allen and June Cull, Beaminster, Dorset
Gerald and Margaret Cummins, Beaminster (1954-1997)
Mr and Mrs Colin Cuthbert, Beaminster
Helen Cutler, Worthing, West Sussex
Anne-Marie Davey, Beaminster, Dorset
Olga Davidson
Dennis G. Denning, Queensferry
Mavis and Pat Diment, Beaminster, Dorset
Mark Diment, Beaminster, Dorset
Andrew Diment, Weymouth, Dorset
Geoffrey J. Dimmock and Caroline Dimmock, Beaminster, Dorset
Bernard J. Doble, Broadwindsor, Dorset
Mrs Helen Doble (née Crabb), Blackdown, Beaminster
Dorset History Centre, Dorchester
A. Douglas, Beaminster, Dorset
Judith Drew, Wootton-under-Edge, Glos
Mrs N. Duce, Woodbridge Close, Heanor, Derbyshire
Adrian Dunford, Beaminster, Dorset
Brian Dunford, Beaminster, Dorset
Mrs Dorothy Earl, Beaminster, Dorset

Joe and Connie Edwards, Banstead, Surrey
Joan and John. R. Edwards, Beaminster, Dorset
John and Barbara Eedle, Beaminster
Toby Eeles, Mosterton, Dorset
Yvonne A. Eley (née Pomeroy), Beaminster
Mrs Brenda Erscott, Halstock
Chris and June Etherington, Beaminster
Denise Evans, Beaminster, Dorset
Major M.A. Everitt, Beaminster
Ron and Valerie Fairbairn, Beaminster
Mrs Brenda Farrance, Thorpebay, Essex
Jessica and Matthew Fawkes, Ruislip, Middlesex
P.R. Field, Bramber, West Sussex
Lynette Fisher, Le Vieux Four
Colin Forsey, Beaminster
Mrs Trixie Frampton, Chedington
Peggy A. Frew, Beaminster
Mr and Mrs M. J. Furber, Lyme Regis, Dorset
Roy and Anita Fursey, Netherbury, Dorset
Chris Gale, Beaminster, Dorset
David Gardner, Axminster
Mrs Mary L. Gardner, Beaminster
Mr and Mrs Robert Garrett,
Mrs Geraldine Gasparelli, Carshalton, Surrey
Barry and Jean Gibbs, Bridport, Dorset
Mike Gibbs, Philadelphia, USA
Maurice A. T. Gibbs, Beaminster
Colin Gibbs, Cheam, Surrey
Catherine M. Gilgrist, Burntwood, Staffs
Mr and Mrs S.W. Gilman, Ontario, Canada
Beryl Gomme, Beaminster
David F. and Alastair J. Grain, Chandlers Ford,
    Hants
Mark A. Greenham, Beaminster
Mark and Louise Greenham, Beaminster, Dorset
Tony V. Greenham, Beaminster
Derek and Kathleen Greenwood, Beaminster, Dorset
Sharon M. Greig, Beaminster, Dorset
John and Maureen Grenville, Beaminster
Harry and Helen Grenville, Frampton
Mark Griffin, Beaminster, Dorset
Irwin and Sally Gunning, Bedford
Frank W. Guppy, Cheltenham
John Hallett, Beaminster
M. J. Hann
Edward J. Hann, Orton Malborne, Peterborough
Chris Hann, Fareham, Hants
Marjorie M. Harborough M.B.E., Beaminster
Philip and Sarah Hardwill, Blackdown, Beaminster
Professor and Mrs Duncan Harris, Beaminster,
    Dorset
Mrs Anne Harris, Wilmslow, Cheshire
Mary Haskett (née Ascott), Beaminster
Maureen Heal, Yeovil, Somerset
Mrs S.F. Heasman, Llantwit Major, Wales
Simon Hedworth, Beaminster
Ross Hendry, The Book Shop, Bridport
Patricia A. Hewitt, Hooke, Dorset
Benita and Adrian Hiley, Grove, Wantage, Oxford

Mark Hill, Beaminster, Dorset
Colin and June Hill, Nailsea, North Somerset
Gwen Hill (née Greening), Xylophagou, Cyprus
Nelson Hillier, Beaminster, Dorset
David and Susan Hine, Eaton, Oxfordshire
D.M. Hine, Beaminster
Margaret A. Hiney, Beaminster, Dorset
Kenneth G. Hoare, Beaminster, Dorset
R. T. Hodder, East Coker
Joan Holland, Beaminster
Mr Mark Hooper and Miss Evelyn Doble,
    Hollymoor Lane, Beaminster
Robert and Adele Hounsell, Burridge House,
    Chardstock
Norman G. House, Beaminster, Dorset
Mrs Ann Hudson, Beaminster
Joyce Hughes, Beaminster
Mrs P. Hunt, 25 East Street, Beaminster, Dorset
Lucy Hunt (Auntie), Beaminster
Stanley Hurford, Beaminster
Michael Hussey, Beaminster, Dorset
D. John Hussey, Beaminster, Dorset
D.C.M. Hutchings
Robert Jasper, Beaminster
Mrs Y. Jeans, Loughbourgh
Mr J. Jeans, Wisconson, USA
Chris and Valerie Jepps, Beaminster
Pat and Ian Johnson, Hooke, Dorset
Mr Lessel R. Jones, Beaminster, Dorset
Fraser and Sarah Keen, Beaminster, Dorset
John Kemp, Beaminster, Dorset
Prof. C.R. Kennedy, Beaminster, Dorset
Kitson & Trotman Solicitors, Beaminster
Jill D. Knights, South Perrott, Dorset
John Learmont, Beaminster, Dorset
David Legg, Netherbury, Bridport
Mr and Mrs Lester, Beaminster
Jude Lewin, Chetnole, Dorset
Max Lewis, Bridport, Dorset
James C. Lill, Bridport, Dorset
Mr and Mrs Michael Lomax, Bridport Road,
    Beaminster
Mr and Mrs C. Longridge
Roger and Gillian Lovegrove, Bookham, Surrey
David L. Lowcock, Solicitor, Kitson & Trotman,
    Beaminster
Sylvia Lymbery, Beaminster and Oxford
Nicola and Heini Maag, Zurich
Mr A.J. Mackinnon
Viscount Marchwood (Penny), Chedington
Mr and Mrs M.J. Marsh, Suffolk
Robert W. McCarthy, Burwell, Cambs
Mr and Mrs R.J. Meech, Bridport
Elizabeth J. Meech, Dorchester, Dorset
Brian J. Moore
Derek Neal
Anne and Martin Newbury, Beaminster, Dorset
Kenneth Newman, Chedington
Wendy S.E. Nicholls, Kidderminster, Worcs

SUBSCRIBERS

Sonia and Michael Nitti, Hardington Moor,
	Somerset
Sylvie and Delia Norris, Melplash, Dorset
Christine O'Connor, Costa Mesa, California
Canon Gregory Page-Turner, Beaminster, Dorset
Mrs Jean Palmer, Marshwood, Dorset
Edward and Edna Pannell, Hereford
Betty and John Patrick, Beaminster, Dorset
Mrs Diane Payne, Beaminster
Johnny and Caroline Payne, Beaminster
Robin and Sheila Pearce, Mosterton
Bob and Margaret Pearson, Beaminster
R.N.R. Peers, Beaminster
Delise Pollard, Farnham, Surrey
Alfred B.H. Pomeroy, Portsmouth (née Beaminster)
Mary Poole
Steve and Maureen Poole, Bournemouth
Mr and Mrs J. Poole, Holymoor Lane, Beaminster
Bridget P. Pountney, Kidderminster, Worcs
Roy A. Pueschner, Beaminster, Dorset
Norman Edward Purchase
Shirley Pye (née Tolman), Beaminster
Peter and Diana Riglar, Bradpole, Dorset
Jacqueline E. Riley, Wareham, Dorset
R.J. Roberts
David and June Rose, Solihull, West Midlands
Duncan Rose, Bridport, Dorset
Murray and Jane Rose, Beaminster, Dorset
Robbie Roskell, Netherbury, Dorset
Matthew Roskell, Beaminster, Dorset
Penelope Ruddock,, Beaminster
Lesley and Patrick Rundle, Beaminster
Shirley and Stuart Salt, Englefield Green, Surrey
Brian and Maureen Sammons, Beaminster, Dorset
Frederick J. Scadding, Bridport, Dorset
Sheila M.A. Scadding, Beaminster, Dorset
Betty M. Scammell (née Newton), Ash, Surrey
Sue and Tony Scott, Beaminster
Ray Scovell, Bridport, Dorset
Phillip J. Scovell, Beaminster, Dorset
Dr and Mrs George Sewell, Macclesfield, Cheshire
Michael J. Shiner, Great Malvern, Worcs
Roger Skilton, Leyburn, North Yorkshire
Mrs April Skinner, Eastwood, Essex
Colin and Celia Smith, Beaminster
Dorothy Snook (née Swaffield)
Betty Spencer (née Hooper)

N. and J. Stephenson, Beaminster, Dorset
A.J. and R.E. Stocks, Beaminster
Monica Stokes (née Hooper)
Gil Streets M.B.E., Beaminster
Elizabeth Stuckey, Halstock, Dorset
Eunice Sutherland, Beaminster, Dorset
Bernard Thorpe, Beaminster, Dorset
Michael Tolman, Beaminster
Winifred May Tompkins, Beaminster
Elizabeth M. Toogood, Long Bredy, Dorset
Cecilia Toohill (née Mason), Beaminster
Mrs Brenda Travers
Mary Treacher, Beaminster, Dorset
Margaret R. Trenchard (née Turner),
David George Trevett, Hyde, Netherbury, Bridport
Mr F. and Mrs B. Trotman, Dorchester, Dorset
Dr and Mrs T. Trower, Yetminster, Dorset
Anthony J. Trumbell, London
Michael Turner, Oakfield, Poole, Dorset
Ian Turner, West Bay, Dorset
Herbert/E.J. Turner, Netherbury
Hilda M. Wait (née Newton), Ninfield, East Sussex
Anne M. Walbridge, Newport, S. Wales
John M. Walbridge, Woodford, Northants
Mary Walbridge, Beaminster, Dorset
Evelyn R. Walden, Beaminster, Dorset
John F.W. Walling, Newton Abbot, Devon
Jeromy Ward, Beaminster, Dorset
Mrs Daphne Warner, Beaminster
A. J. Warren, West Bay, Dorset
John Watt, Beaminster, Dorset
Fred Waygood, Stafford
Webb Family, Cerne Abbas, Dorset
Audrey Welsford (née Pidgeon), Beaminster
Benjamin Westgarth, Sill, Beaminster
Peter Westgarth, Sill, U.S.A
Natalie Wheatley (née Swaffield)
Yvonne Widger, Beaminster
Elizabeth L. Wiles, Beaminster, Dorset
Mrs Joan E. Wilkinson, Melplash, Dorset
Annette and John Willis, Horn Hill View
Mr and Mrs R.M. Wilson, Beaminster
Mrs Patrica Bishop Windsor, Wem, (Grand Daughter
	Bishops, Clay Lane, Beaminster [Wheel Wright])
Steve and Julie Wood, Beaminster, Dorset
Peter James Woodbury, Drimpton, Beaminster
Choi Keum Yul, Paju City, South Korea

Further Titles

For information regarding up-to-date availability, please check our website at www.halsgrove.com

✦ FURTHER TITLES ✦

The Book of Herne Hill • Patricia Jenkyns

The Book of Hethersett • Hethersett Society
Research Group

The Book of High Bickington • Avril Stone

The Book of Homersfield • Ken Palmer

The Book of Honiton • Gerald Gosling

The Book of Ilsington • Dick Wills

The Book of Kessingland • Maureen and Eric Long

The Book of Kingskerswell • Carsewella Local
History Group

The Book of Lamerton • Ann Cole and Friends

Lanner, A Cornish Mining Parish • Sharron
Schwartz and Roger Parker

The Book of Leigh & Bransford • Malcolm Scott

The Second Book of Leigh & Bransford • Malcolm Scott

The Book of Litcham with Lexham & Mileham • Litcham
Historical and Amenity Society

The Book of Llangain • Haydn Williams

The Book of Loddiswell • Loddiswell Parish History Group

The Book of Looe • Mark Camp

The New Book of Lostwithiel • Barbara Fraser

The Book of Lulworth • Rodney Legg

The Book of Lustleigh • Joe Crowdy

The Book of Lydford • Compiled by Barbara Weeks

The Book of Lyme Regis • Rodney Legg

The Book of Manaton • Compiled by the People
of the Parish

The Book of Markyate • Markyate Local History Society

The Book of Mawnan • Mawnan Local History Group

The Book of Meavy • Pauline Hemery

The Book of Mere • Dr David Longbourne

The Book of Minehead with Alcombe • Binding and Stevens

The Book of Monks Orchard and Eden Park • Ian Muir
and Pat Manning

The Book of Morchard Bishop • Jeff Kingaby

Mount Batten – The Flying Boats of Plymouth •
Gerald Wasley

The Book of Mulbarton • Jill and David Wright

The Book of Mylor • Mylor Local History Group

The Book of Narborough • Narborough Local
History Society

The Book of Newdigate • John Callcut

The Book of Newtown • Keir Foss

The Book of Nidderdale • Nidderdale Museum Society

The Book of Northlew with Ashbury • Northlew
History Group

The Book of North Newton • J.C. and K.C. Robins

The Book of North Tawton • Baker, Hoare and Shields

The Book of Notting Hill • Melvin Wilkinson

The Book of Nynehead • Nynehead & District
History Society

The Book of Okehampton • Roy and Ursula Radford

The Book of Ottery St Mary • Gerald Gosling and
Peter Harris

The Book of Paignton • Frank Pearce

The Book of Penge, Anerley & Crystal Palace •
Peter Abbott

The Book of Peter Tavy with Cudlipptown • Peter Tavy
Heritage Group

The Book of Pimperne • Jean Coull

The Book of Plymtree • Tony Eames

The Book of Poole • Rodney Legg

The Book of Porchfield & Locks Green • Keir Foss

The Book of Porlock • Dennis Corner

The Book of Portland • Rodney Legg

Postbridge – The Heart of Dartmoor • Reg Bellamy

The Book of Priddy • Albert Thompson

The Book of Princetown • Dr Gardner-Thorpe

The Book of Probus • Alan Kent and
Danny Merrifield

The Book of Rattery • By the People of the Parish

The Book of Roadwater, Leighland and Treborough •
Clare and Glyn Court

The Book of St Audries • Duncan Stafford

The Book of St Austell • Peter Hancock

The Book of St Day • Joseph Mills and Paul Annear

The Book of St Dennis and Goss Moor • Kenneth Rickard

The Book of St Ervan • Moira Tangye

The Book of St Levan • St Levan Local History Group

The Book of St Mawes • Chris Pollard

*The Book of Sampford Courtenay
with Honeychurch* • Stephanie Pouya

The Book of Sculthorpe • Gary Windeler

The Book of Seaton • Ted Gosling

The Book of Sennen • Alison Weeks and
Valerie Humphrys

The Book of Sidmouth • Ted Gosling and Sheila Luxton

The Book of Silverton • Silverton Local History Society

The Book of South Molton • Jonathan Edmunds

The Book of South Stoke with Midford • Edited by
Robert Parfitt

South Tawton & South Zeal with Sticklepath • Roy and
Ursula Radford

The Book of Sparkwell with Hemerdon & Lee Mill • Pam James

159